OTHER PLANETS

OTHER PLANETS

The Portable New Century Edition

EMANUEL SWEDENBORG

Translated from the Latin by George F. Dole
and Jonathan S. Rose

SWEDENBORG FOUNDATION
West Chester, Pennsylvania

Originally published in Latin as *De Telluribus in Mundo Nostro Solari, Quae Vocantur Planetae, et de Telluribus in Coelo Astrifero, deque Illarum Incolis, Tum de Spiritibus et Angelis Ibi: Ex Auditis et Visis,* London, 1758.

Printed in the United States of America

ISBN (portable)   978-0-87785-417-3
ISBN (e-book of portable edition) 978-0-87785-682-5
This translation is also included in the hardcover library edition of *The Shorter Works of 1758,* ISBN 978-0-87785-482-1.

Library of Congress Cataloging-in-Publication Data

Names: Swedenborg, Emanuel, 1688–1772, author. | Dole, George F., translator. | Rose, Jonathan S., 1956– translator.
Title: Other planets / Emanuel Swedenborg ; translated from the Latin by George F. Dole and Jonathan S. Rose.
Other titles: De telluribus in mundo nostro solari. English
Description: The portable new century edition. | West Chester, Pennsylvania : Swedenborg Foundation, 2018. | "Originally published in Latin as De Telluribus in Mundo Nostro Solari, Quae Vocantur Planetae, et de Telluribus in Coelo Astrifero, deque Illarum Incolis, Tum de Spiritibus et Angelis Ibi: Ex Auditis et Visis, London, 1758." | Includes bibliographical references.
Identifiers: LCCN 2014050013 | ISBN 9780877854173 (pbk. : alk. paper)
Subjects: LCSH: Cosmology—Early works to 1800.
Classification: LCC BX8712 .E3 2018 | DDC 289/.4—dc23
LC record available at https://lccn.loc.gov/2014050013

Senior copy editor, Alicia L. Dole
Text designed by Joanna V. Hill
Ornaments from the first Latin edition, 1758
Typesetting by Alicia L. Dole
Cover designed by Karen Connor

For information contact:
Swedenborg Foundation
320 North Church Street
West Chester, PA 19380 USA
Telephone: (610) 430-3222
Web: www.swedenborg.com
E-mail: info@swedenborg.com

Contents

Conventions Used in This Work

MOST of the following conventions apply generally to the translations in the New Century Edition Portable series. For introductory material on the content and history of *Other Planets,* and for annotations on the subject matter, including obscure or problematic content, and extensive indexes, the reader is referred to the Deluxe New Century Edition volume *The Shorter Works of 1758.*

Section numbers Following a practice common in his time, Swedenborg divided his published theological works into sections numbered in sequence from beginning to end. His original section numbers have been preserved in this edition; they appear in boxes in the outside margins. Traditionally, these sections have been referred to as "numbers" and designated by the abbreviation "n." In this edition, however, the more common section symbol (§) is used to designate the section numbers, and the sections are referred to as such.

Subsection numbers Because many sections throughout Swedenborg's works are too long for precise cross-referencing, Swedenborgian scholar John Faulkner Potts (1838–1923) further divided them into subsections; these have since become standard, though minor variations occur from one edition to another. These subsections are indicated by bracketed numbers that appear in the text itself: [2], [3], and so on. Because the beginning of the first *subsection* always coincides with the beginning of the *section* proper, it is not labeled in the text.

Citations of Swedenborg's text As is common in Swedenborgian studies, text citations of Swedenborg's works refer not to page numbers but to section numbers, which unlike page numbers are uniform in most editions. In citations the section symbol (§) is generally omitted after the title of a work by Swedenborg. Thus "*Secrets of Heaven* 6393" would refer to section 6393 (§6393) of Swedenborg's *Secrets of Heaven,* not to page 6393 of any edition. Subsection numbers are given after a colon; a reference such as "§6393:2" would indicate subsection 2 of section 6393. The reference "6393:1" would indicate the first subsection of section 6393, though that subsection is not in fact labeled in the text. Where section numbers stand alone without titles, their function is indicated by the prefixed section symbol; for example, "§6393:2". However, section marks are generally omitted in Swedenborg's indexlike references to *Secrets of Heaven.*

Citations of the Bible Biblical citations in this edition follow the accepted standard: a semicolon is used between book references and between chapter references, and a comma between verse references. Therefore "Matthew 5:11, 12; 6:1; 10:41, 42; Luke 6:23, 35" refers to Matthew chapter 5, verses 11 and 12; Matthew chapter 6, verse 1; Matthew chapter 10, verses 41 and 42; and Luke chapter 6, verses 23 and 35. Swedenborg often incorporated the numbers of verses not actually represented in his text when listing verse numbers for a passage he quoted; these apparently constitute a kind of "see also" reference to other material he felt was relevant, and are generally retained in this edition. This edition also follows Swedenborg where he cites contiguous verses individually (for example, John 1:1, 2, 3, 4), rather than as a range (John 1:1–4). Occasionally this edition supplies a full, conventional Bible reference where Swedenborg omits one after a quotation.

Quotations in Swedenborg's works Some features of the original Latin text of *Other Planets* have been modernized in this edition. For example, Swedenborg's first edition generally relies on context or italics rather than on quotation marks to indicate passages taken from the Bible or from other works. The manner in which these conventions are used in the original suggests that Swedenborg did not feel it necessary to belabor the distinction between direct quotation and paraphrase of the Bible; but in this edition, directly quoted material is indicated by either block quotations or quotation marks, and paraphrased material is presented without such indicators. In passages of dialog as well, quotation marks have been introduced that were not present as such in the original. Furthermore, Swedenborg did not mark his omissions from or changes to material he quoted, a practice in which this edition generally follows him.

Swedenborg's footnotes The author's footnotes, indicated by superscript letters in the main body of the text, consist of cross-references to his previously published *Secrets of Heaven* (1749–1756). It should be observed that Swedenborg's general practice was to use the lettering series *a–z, aa–zz,* and *aaa–zzz* before starting over at *a,* whereas in this edition the lettering starts over after each chapter heading.

Changes to and insertions in the text This translation is based on the first Latin edition, published by Swedenborg himself. It incorporates the silent emendation of minor errors, not only in the text proper but in Bible verse references and in section references to Swedenborg's other published theological works. The text has also been changed without notice where the verse numbering of the Latin Bible cited by Swedenborg differs from that of modern English Bibles. Throughout the translation, references or cross-references that were implied but not stated have been inserted in square brackets [ ]; for example, [Luke 24:39], [*Secrets of Heaven* 1110, 2784, 6393]. By contrast, references that appear in parentheses reflect references that occur in the first edition; for example, (1 Samuel 30:16), (see §42 above). Words not occurring in the first Latin edition, but necessary for the understanding of the text, also appear in square brackets; this device has been used sparingly, however, even at the risk of some inconsistency in its application.

Chapter numbering Swedenborg did not number the chapters of *Other Planets*. His decision not to do so seems to have been deliberate, and in accord with it chapter numbers are not included in the text. However, because some studies of his works make reference to chapter numbers, the table of contents provides them.

Problematic content Occasionally Swedenborg makes statements that, although mild by the standards of eighteenth-century theological discourse, now read as harsh, dismissive, or insensitive. The most problematic are assertions about or criticisms of various religious traditions and their adherents—including Judaism, ancient or contemporary; Roman Catholicism; Islam; and the Protestantism in which Swedenborg himself grew up. These statements are far outweighed in size and importance by other passages in Swedenborg's works earnestly maintaining the value of every individual and of all religions. This wider context is discussed in the introductions and annotations of the Deluxe edition mentioned above. In the present format, however, problematic statements must be retained without comment. The other option—to omit them—would obscure some aspects of Swedenborg's presentation and in any case compromise its historicity.

The Earthlike Bodies

Called

Planets

in Our Solar System

and

in Deep Space,

Their Inhabitants,

and

the Spirits and Angels There

Drawn from Things Heard and Seen

The Planets in the Universe

BY the Lord's divine mercy the deeper levels within me, which belong I
to my spirit, have been opened, enabling me to talk with spirits and
angels—not only those near our world, but also those close to other planets.
Because I have had a longing to know whether there are other worlds, what
they are like, and what their inhabitants are like, the Lord has granted me
opportunities to talk and interact with spirits and angels from other planets. With some of them I spent all day, with others a full week, and with
still others months on end. I learned from them about the planets they
came from and are close to now, about the life, customs, and worship of
the inhabitants of those planets, and various other noteworthy details about
them. Since it has been granted to me to know such things in this way, I
am in a position to offer descriptions based on things I myself have heard
and seen.

[2] It is important to know that all spirits and angels are human[a]
and that they remain close to their planet of origin.[b] They know what is

---

The statements immediately following, and those printed below the lines
on subsequent pages, are explained and illustrated in [the indicated sections of] *Secrets of Heaven.*

a. There is no such thing as spirits and angels who are not human: 1880.
b. The spirits from each planet remain close to that planet, because they once lived there themselves, they have a nature similar to that of the current inhabitants, and the inhabitants need their
help: 9968.

happening on that planet; and any people whose deeper levels have been opened to the point where they can talk and interact with spirits and angels can learn such things from those spirits and angels. After all, in our essence we too are spirits;[c] and in our deeper levels we are already among other spirits.[d] So anyone whose deeper levels have been opened by the Lord can talk with spirits and angels the way people talk with each other.[e] For twelve years now, this has been granted to me daily.

 In the other life it is common knowledge that there are many planets with people on them and consequently spirits and angels from them. If a love of truth and therefore some useful reason prompts people there to want to talk with spirits from other worlds, they are all allowed to do so. This assures them that there is indeed a plurality of worlds and informs them that humankind exists on not just one earth but countless planets. It teaches them also about the character and life of these people, and about their worship of God.

I have talked with spirits from our earth about this a number of times. We concluded that anyone with a capable mind can see, on the basis of things that are well known, that there must be many planets and they must have people on them. That is, we can determine on rational grounds that bodies as large as the planets—and some of them are significantly larger than our own—are not uninhabited lumps created only to be carried along on a wandering course around the Sun and shed their feeble light for the benefit of just one planet. Their function must be more worthwhile than this.

If we believe, as everyone should, that the Divine created the universe for the sole purpose of bringing humankind into being as the source of heaven (because humankind is the seedbed of heaven), then we cannot help but believe that wherever there is a planet there must be people on it.

---

c. The soul that lives after death is our spirit, which is the essential person within us; in the other life it appears in a perfect human form: 322, 1880, 1881, 3633, 4622, 4735, 6054, 6605, 6626, 7021, 10594.

d. Even while we are in this world, in our deeper levels, meaning our spirit or soul, we are surrounded by spirits and angels whose character is like our own: 2379, 3644, 4067, 4073, 4077.

e. It is possible for us to talk with spirits and angels; the early people on our planet did this frequently: 67, 68, 69, 784, 1634, 1636, 7802. These days, however, it is dangerous to talk with them unless we have true faith and are being led by the Lord: 784, 9438, 10751.

[2] As for the objects visible to our eyes because they are within our solar system, we can obviously tell that they are planets from the fact that they are bodies of physical matter. They reflect the light of the Sun, and when we look at them through a telescope they do not look like stars, which twinkle because of their fire, but appear earthlike, with darker and lighter patches. There is also the fact that they, like our own planet, travel around the Sun along the path of the zodiac, which must cause years and the seasons of the year called spring, summer, fall, and winter. Similarly, they rotate on their axes as our planet does, which must cause days and the times of day called morning, afternoon, evening, and night. Not only that, some of them have moons called satellites, which have their own periodic orbits around their sphere the way our moon orbits our planet. The planet Saturn, which is very far from the Sun, has a huge luminous ring around it that gives a great deal of light to that planet, even though it is reflected light. Can any rational individual who knows all this maintain that these bodies are uninhabited?

Further, I have talked with spirits about the fact that if people consider how incredibly vast the starry heaven is and how incalculably huge the number of stars in it is—and each star is a sun in its own realm, has its own solar system, and is much like our sun, though it may vary from it in magnitude—they can come to believe there is more than one inhabited world in the universe. Anyone who ponders this in the right way will conclude that all this immensity must be a means of achieving the ultimate purpose of creation, which is a heavenly kingdom in which the Divine can dwell with angels and with people [still in the physical world]. The whole visible universe, the sky studded with stars beyond number, each and every one of which is a sun, is just a means of producing planets with people on them, people who are the source of that heavenly kingdom. **4**

The only conclusion rational individuals can draw from this is that a means so vast for a purpose so great was not brought into being so that a single planet could then produce the human race and the heaven it populates. How would that satisfy the Divine, which is infinite, for which thousands or even millions of planets full of people would amount to so little a thing as to be almost nothing?

Not only that, the angelic heaven is as vast as it is in order to correspond to the details of the human body, and there are millions of details **5** involved in each of its members, organs, and viscera and in every condition it goes through. I have been given to understand that, seen in the light of these correspondences, heaven could not exist at all if it did not consist of people from a great many different planets.[f]

6   There are some spirits whose sole interest is in gathering information. Since nothing else gives them pleasure, they are allowed to travel around even to other solar systems beyond this one and acquire knowledge for themselves. They have reported that not only are there planets within this solar system that are inhabited, there are inhabited planets around other stars as well, in fact a huge number of them.

The spirits who learned this were from the planet Mercury.

7   As for the worship of God by the inhabitants of other planets, generally speaking any who are not idolaters acknowledge the Lord as the only God. That is, they worship the Divine not as a God who cannot be seen but as a God who can be seen, because the Divine, when appearing to them, appears in a human form, a form like that seen long ago by Abraham and others on this planet;[g] and everyone who worships the Divine in human form is accepted by the Lord.[h]

Such people also say that no one can properly worship God, let alone be joined to him, who does not have some understandable concept of him, and that God can be understood only in human form. Otherwise the inner sight we direct at God, the sight of our thinking, loses all coherence the way our eyesight does when it tries to focus on the limitless vastness of the universe. Our thinking then cannot help but sink down into a focus on the physical world and worship it instead of God.

---

f. Heaven corresponds to the Lord, and a human individual in every detail corresponds to heaven, so in the Lord's sight heaven in its full representation is a human being, and should be referred to as the universal human: 2996, 2998, 3624–3649, 3741–3745, 4625. An overview from personal experience of the way in which a human in all respects corresponds to the universal human that is heaven: 3021, 3624–3649, 3741–3750, 3883–3896, 4039–4055, 4218–4228, 4318–4331, 4403–4421, 4527–4533, 4622–4634, 4652–4660, 4791–4805, 4931–4953, 5050–5062, 5171–5189, 5377–5395, 5552–5573, 5711–5727, 10030.

g. The inhabitants of all planets worship the Divine in human form, which means that they are worshiping the Lord: 8541–8547, 10159, 10736, 10737, 10738. They rejoice when they hear that God actually became a human being: 9361. Our thinking about God goes nowhere unless we think of God as existing in a human form: 8705, 9359, 9972. We can worship and love an entity of which we can form some mental image, but not an entity of which we can form no mental image: 4733, 5110, 5663, 7211, 9356, 10067, 10267.

h. The Lord accepts everyone who is devoted to doing some good and who worships the Divine in human form: 7173, 9359.

When [spirits from other planets] were told that the Lord put on a human nature in our world, they thought it over a little and soon said that this happened for the sake of the salvation of humankind. **8**

The Planet *Mercury* and Its Spirits and Inhabitants

ONE of the secrets not yet known in this world is that heaven in its entirety is like one individual, which is therefore called the universal human, and that absolutely everything in us, on both our inner and outer levels, corresponds to something in that universal human, or heaven. I have demonstrated this many times elsewhere, though.[a] **9**

Not enough people come into heaven from our world to make up that universal human. We are relatively few, so people from many other planets are needed as well. As a result, the Lord has provided that the moment there is any deficiency anywhere in the quality or quantity of people needed to embody this correspondence, people from another planet are immediately summoned to fill the need, so that the proper proportion is maintained and heaven therefore stands firm.

What spirits from the planet Mercury relate to in the universal human has been disclosed to me by a heavenly source. It is the function of memory, but specifically the memory of abstract concepts, apart from things that are earthly and merely physical. **10**

Since it has been granted to me to talk with the spirits of Mercury for many weeks and hear about their nature and explore what things are like for the people who live on that planet, I wish to relate my experiences with them.

Some spirits came to me, and I was told by a heavenly source that they were from the planet closest to the Sun, which in our world is called Mercury. As soon as they reached me, they searched my memory to see **11**

---

a. See note f on §5.

what I knew. This is something spirits can do most skillfully, because when they come close to an individual they can see what is in that individual's memory in detail.[b] As they were going through various things in my memory, including the cities and places I had been to, I noticed that they had no interest in knowing about the churches or palaces or houses or streets I had seen but only what I knew had happened in those locations, as well as what form of government existed there, and what the character and customs of the citizens were, and things like that. In our memories such matters are associated with particular places, so when the places are called to mind, these characteristics come to mind as well.

I was surprised that the spirits were like this, so I asked them why they had no interest in the magnificent things that exist in those places, but instead wished to know only about the culture and events there. They said that they found pleasure only in looking at what is real, and none in looking at material, physical, or earthly things. This gave me confirmation that in the universal human the spirits from that planet relate to the memory of things that are apart from what is physical and earthly.

12 I was told that this attitude also shapes how the inhabitants of that planet live. That is, they are completely uninterested in earthly and bodily things but are very interested in the statutes, laws, and forms of government of the peoples who live there. They are also interested in the information they have about heaven, which is abundant. I was told that many of the people on that planet talk with spirits and learn from them about spiritual realities and about different states of life after death. This too has led them to disregard bodily and earthly matters. Once people really know about life after death and believe in it, heavenly things are of great interest to them, because these last forever and bring happiness; but they care nothing for worldly things, except as far as the necessities of life require them.

Since this is what the inhabitants of that planet are like, this is also the nature of the spirits who come from there.[c]

13 I could tell how eagerly they seek out and soak up all types of knowledge retained in the part of the memory that transcends the physical senses by this: in the course of investigating what I knew about heaven and running

---

b. Spirits have access to everything in our memory, but nothing can pass from their memory into ours: 2488, 5853, 6192, 6193, 6198, 6199, 6214. Angels have access to the desires and goals in us that give rise to and determine the precise ways in which we think, will, and act: 1317, 1645, 5854.
c. See note b on §1.

through it all, they kept saying, "That's right. That's right." As I just mentioned, when spirits come to someone they gain access to everything in that individual's memory, and retrieve from it whatever suits their interests. In fact, they read what is there like a book, a phenomenon I have often observed.[d]

These spirits were doing all this with extraordinary skill and speed because they were not dwelling on types of information that are heavy and sluggish, which constrain and therefore slow down inner sight. All that is earthly and bodily has this dulling effect when we focus on it, which is what we do when it is the only thing we love. Instead, these spirits pay attention to higher information. Concepts that have nothing earthly clinging to them lift the mind up and give it a panoramic view, while information that focuses on what is merely physical drags the mind down, hemming it in and closing it.

The following experience, too, showed me how intensely eager they are to gather higher types of knowledge and enrich their memory with them. I was writing at one point about things yet to come, and they were too far away to see the contents of my memory. Because I was unwilling to read out loud to them what I had written, they became intensely annoyed and, going against their usual principles, attempted to assault me verbally, saying that I was a terrible person and things like that. To show how angry they were, they also brought about a painful kind of pressure on the right side of my head, from the crown to the ear. That sort of thing did no harm at all to me, but because what they had done was wrong, they moved farther away from me. Even so, they soon stopped in their tracks, because they were still longing to know what I had written. That is how great their passion for learning is.

The spirits from Mercury possess far more knowledge than other spirits do, both about what is going on within our own solar system and also about what is happening on extrasolar planets. Once they have learned something they retain it, and they also recall it every time they encounter something similar. This shows that spirits have the faculty of memory and that their memory is far better than ours is. It also shows that spirits retain what they hear and see and perceive, especially things they enjoy, such as the information about higher realities that gives pleasure to these

14

---

d. The spirits who are with someone adopt everything in that person's memory: 5853, 5857, 5858, 5859.

spirits from Mercury. This is because things that we delight in and love flow into us almost effortlessly and remain with us. The rest does not penetrate but only glances off the surface of our minds and disappears.

15 When spirits from Mercury come to other communities [in the spiritual world] they investigate what the inhabitants there know, and once they have learned it, they leave. The sharing of information among spirits, and especially among angels, is such that when they visit a community, if they are loved and well received, they share in everything its residents know.[e]

16 Because of their wealth of knowledge, spirits from Mercury have more pride than other spirits have, so they were told that no matter how much they know, there is infinitely more that they do not know, and if their knowledge kept increasing forever they still could not attain to even a rough notion of everything in general. They were told that they are susceptible to pride and to a high opinion of themselves, and that this is unseemly. They replied that it is not pride; it is just a glorying in their faculty of memory. So this is how they excuse their faults.

17 They have a distaste for verbal speech because it is a physical thing, so if there were no mediating spirits present, the only way I was able to talk with them was through a kind of active thinking.

Since their memory retains concepts rather than purely physical images, it more readily supplies subject matter to their thoughts, because on the level of thinking that transcends mere mental imaging, the objects of thought are things that have been stripped of their materiality. Yet even though this is the case, spirits from Mercury have very little skill in the exercise of judgment. They take no pleasure in exercising judgment or drawing conclusions from what they have learned. Knowledge by itself is their delight.

18 I asked them whether they did not want to make some use of their knowledge, because taking delight in knowledge is not enough. After all, knowledge exists to serve some use, and usefulness has to be its goal. By itself what they know does them no good, I said, although it might be helpful to others, if these spirits were willing to share what they know. If someone wants to become wise, it is not at all effective to stay focused

---

e. In the heavens everything that is good is shared, because heavenly love shares everything it has with others; and this is the basis of angels' wisdom and happiness: 549, 550, 1390, 1391, 10130, 10723.

only on having knowledge, because knowledge is no more than an instrumental means that helps us in our search for the way we ought to live. They answered, though, that they truly enjoy learning and that for them it is in fact useful just to know things.

Some of them actually did not want to look like people the way spirits from other planets do, but like crystal balls instead. The reason they wanted to look like this even though they did not is that in the other life knowledge that transcends what is physical is represented by crystals. **[19]**

The spirits from Mercury are completely different from the spirits from our planet, because the spirits from our planet attach no value to anything except what is worldly, physical, and earthly—what is made of matter. This means that spirits from Mercury cannot be together with spirits from our planet; wherever they encounter spirits from our planet, they beat a hasty retreat. The spiritual auras that radiate from each are almost exactly opposite. **[20]**

Spirits from Mercury are fond of saying that they have no interest in looking at the husk but only at things stripped of their husk—deeper things, that is.

I kept seeing a fairly bright, cheerful flame for the better part of an hour. The flame signaled the arrival of some other spirits from Mercury, but these spirits scrutinized things, thought about them, and communicated even more rapidly than the earlier ones. As soon as they came, they ran through the contents of my memory, but I could not catch what they were observing, because they were so quick. I kept hearing them say, "Yes, that's right." As for what I had seen in the heavens and the world of spirits, they said they already knew that information. I perceived that there was a large group of spirits accompanying them, a little behind [me] on the left, on a level with the back of [my] head. **[21]**

On another occasion I saw a large group of the same kind of spirits, but at some distance from me—in front and a little to the right. They communicated with me from there, but had to use other spirits as intermediaries to do so, because their speech is as quick as thought and is not expressible in normal human language except through the mediation of other spirits. To my surprise, they all spoke together as a group, and yet their communication was extremely fast and well timed. Because many were talking at once, I experienced their speech as coming in waves. It was also striking that even though they were to my right, their communication seemed to glide toward my left eye. This was because the left eye **[22]** corresponds to concepts that are separate from matter; the left eye, then, has to do with intelligence, while the right eye has to do with wisdom.[f]

They grasped and evaluated what they heard with the same quickness with which they spoke, saying, "Yes, that's right" or "No, that's not correct." They made up their minds almost instantly.

23 There was a spirit from another planet who was able to communicate with them quite skillfully because he could talk fluently and rapidly, but who adopted an air of elegance in what he said. In an instant they passed judgment on what he was saying. This one point of his, they said, was expressed too elegantly; that other point, too cleverly. All they were looking for was whether he was telling them anything they did not already know. They had no use for things that as far as they are concerned cloud the issue, which are mainly pretensions to eloquence and erudition, because these hide the true message and substitute mere words, which are only matter-based forms for conveying underlying realities. The speaker keeps the mind focused on the words and wants the words rather than their meaning to be heard, so what is affected is the hearing of the other more than the mind.

24 Spirits of the planet Mercury do not stay in one place, or linger among the communities of spirits from one world, but roam throughout the universe. This is because they relate to our conceptual memory, and this memory needs constant enrichment; so they are allowed to roam around and acquire knowledge for themselves everywhere.

If in the course of their travels, though, they run across spirits who love material things—things that are bodily and earthly—they avoid them and go somewhere else where they do not hear about things like that.

This shows that their minds are elevated above what is sensory and that they are therefore in a more inward light. I was actually able to perceive this when they were near me and communicating with me: I noticed at such times that I was being so drawn away from what is sensory that even the light I was seeing with my eyes became weak and dim.

25 The spirits from that planet travel in regiments in tight formation, and when they gather they form a kind of sphere. They are joined together by

---

f. The eye corresponds to our power of understanding because our understanding is our inner sight and sees things that are not made of matter: 2701, 4410, 4526, 9051, 10569. The sight of the left eye corresponds to seeing truths and therefore corresponds to intelligence, while the sight of the right eye corresponds to seeing the good actions that truth teaches, and therefore corresponds to wisdom: 4410.

the Lord so closely that they act as one being; what each individual knows is communicated to all and what all know is communicated to each individual, just as happens in heaven.g

How I learned that they travel throughout the universe to gather new knowledge was that on one occasion, when I saw them already at a fair distance from me, they communicated with me and said that they were now gathered together and were about to leave the region of this solar system to go out among the stars, where they knew there were people who had no concern for earthly, physical matters but only for matters on a higher level. These were people they wanted to be with.

They said that they themselves did not know where they were going but that they were being taken under the Lord's supervision to a place where they could be taught things which they did not yet know, but which fit well with the knowledge they already had. They also said that they did not know how they had found the friends they were already connected to, but that this too had happened under the Lord's supervision.

Since they travel around the universe and are therefore in a position **26** to know more than others about the solar systems and planets outside our own, I talked with them about this as well. They said that there were a great many planets in the universe with people on them. It bewildered them that some people (people they described as not having much sense) thought that the heaven of an omnipotent God could be made up of spirits and angels who came from one planet only, when in comparison with the omnipotence of God these were so few that they would amount to virtually nothing. In fact, this would be the case even if there were millions of solar systems and millions of planets. They went on to say that they knew many hundreds of thousands of [inhabited] planets in the universe—but still, what was that compared to the Divine, which is infinite?

Some spirits from Mercury were with me while I was writing an expla- **27** nation of the Word's inner meaning. When they noticed what I was writing they said that it was very simplistic and that virtually every expression in it seemed mundane. I replied, though, that nevertheless the people of our planet see what I have written as subtle and lofty, and a lot of it they do not understand. I added that many in our world do not even know that there is an inner self that acts on the outer and causes it to be alive. On the basis of deceptive sensory experience, they have convinced themselves

---

g. See note e on §15.

that life is a property of the body, and this leads the ones who are evil and unbelieving to doubt that there even is a life after death. As for the part of us that will live after our bodies die, they call it the soul rather than the spirit, and they argue about what the soul is and where it is located. They believe that the material body, even though it has been scattered to the four winds, must be reunited with the soul before we can live as people again, and things of that kind.

When the spirits from Mercury heard this, they asked whether people of that sort could ever become angels. I replied that people become angels if they have lived lives devoted to acts of goodness that are inspired by faith and caring. In that case they are no longer focused on things that are external and physical but on things that are internal and spiritual; and when they come into this state they are in fact in a light higher than that of the spirits from Mercury. In order that the spirits from Mercury would know that this was true, they were allowed to talk with an angel in heaven from our planet, one who had been like that while living on earth. The story is continued below [§37].

28 Later on, a long sheet of paper was given to me by some spirits from Mercury. It was irregularly shaped because it was made up of a number of individual pages glued together. It seemed to have typeset printing on it, the kind we have in our world. I asked whether they had that sort of thing in their world and they said that they did not, but that they knew that we had printed pages like that in our world. They did not want to say more than that, but I perceived they were thinking that knowledge in our world exists on paper and not in human minds. In fact, they made jokes about pieces of paper on Earth knowing things that the people there do not know. However, the reality of the situation was explained to them.

After a while they came back and gave me another sheet of paper, also covered with printing like the earlier one, only not untidily stuck together, but neat and clean. They said that they had been further informed that the pages on our planet were like that, and that books were made of them.

29 What has just been said shows very clearly that spirits retain in their memories what they see and hear in the other life and that they can be taught just as they could when they were people on their planet. This means they can learn the teachings of faith and can therefore be perfected. The more inwardly aware spirits and angels are, the more quickly and fully they absorb things and the more perfectly they retain them; and since this goes on forever, we can see that they are constantly increasing in wisdom.

For spirits from Mercury, knowledge about things is constantly growing, but this does not result in growth in wisdom, because although they love conceptual knowledge, which is actually only a means to an end, they do not love the using of that knowledge, which is its purpose.

The nature of spirits from the planet Mercury can also be seen in what follows. It is important to know that all spirits and angels were once humans [living in the physical world]. Humankind is the seedbed of heaven. It is also important to know that the characters of spirits are completely determined by the particular passions and inclinations they had when they were living in the physical world, because every individual's life awaits her or him after death.[h] Since this is the case, we can tell the particular character of the people on any planet from the particular character of the spirits who come from that planet. **30**

Since in the universal human the spirits from Mercury relate to the memory of concepts separate from matter, when anyone is talking with them about things that are earthly, physical, and merely worldly, they are totally unwilling to listen; and if they are compelled to listen they change what they are hearing into something else—for the most part, into the exact opposite—as a means of escape. **31**

To make me absolutely sure about their particular character, I was allowed to represent to them meadows, newly ploughed and planted fields, as well as gardens, forests, and rivers ("representing" things like this means displaying images to others; in the other life images seem alive), but they immediately changed the images. They darkened the meadows and farmlands and by representations of their own filled them with snakes; they darkened the rivers so that the water was no longer clear. When I asked why they were doing this, they said that they did not want to think about that sort of thing but about what is conceptual, which is separate from what is earthly, and especially concepts about the kinds of things that happen in the heavens. **32**

Somewhat later I showed them some larger and smaller birds, typical of the ones we have on our planet, since in the other life it is possible to present living images of such things. When they first saw these images of birds they tried to change them, but then they started enjoying them and became **33**

---

h. In every case, our life stays with us and continues after death: 4227, 7439. The outer levels of our life are kept closed after death and the inner levels of our life are opened: 4314, 5128, 6495. Then each and every bit of our thinking is revealed: 4633, 5128.

calmer. This was because birds mean knowledge of spiritual realities, and a perception of this meaning was flowing into them.[i] So they stopped changing the images and blocking them from their memory.

After that I was allowed to show them a very beautiful garden with many oil lamps on stands. This time they paused and paid attention, because oil lamps on stands mean truths that shine because they reveal what is good.[j]

I could see from this that they were able to stay focused on observations of material things, provided the meaning of those things on a spiritual level was suggested at the same time. This is because the things that are present in the Word's spiritual meaning are not that distant from material things, since material things are used to represent them.

34 I also talked with them about sheep and lambs, but they did not want to hear about things like that since they felt that they were earthly. This was because they did not understand what innocence means, which is what lambs represent. I found this out when I told them that the lambs that are represented in heaven mean innocence,[k] and they said that they did not know what innocence was—they knew it only as a word. This was because they are interested only in conceptual knowledge and not in the useful functions that are the purposes of that knowledge, so they had no inner perception of what innocence is.

35 Some spirits from the planet Mercury came to me who had been sent by others to listen in on the discussions that were going on around me. One of the spirits from our own planet told these envoys that when they were reporting back to those who had sent them they should not say anything but the truth. They should not, as they usually did, give misleading information to their questioners, because if any spirits from our planet did that they would be severely punished. However, the group that was at a distance, the group that had sent the spirits, said that if that was a reason for punishing someone, they should all be punished, because they were so used to doing this that they were incapable of doing anything else. They said that they also did this when they were communicating

---

i. Birds mean thoughts, ideas, spiritual knowledge, and things involving reason or understanding: 40, 745, 776, 778, 866, 988, 991, 5149, 7441; and this varies depending on the genus and species of the bird: 3219.

j. Oil lamps on stands mean truths that shine because they reveal what is good: 4638, 9548, 9783.

k. In heaven and in the Word, lambs mean innocence: 3994, 7840, 10132.

with the inhabitants of their own planet. They did not do it out of any intent to deceive, though, but only to stimulate the inhabitants' desire for knowledge. When they give the inhabitants misleading information and hide in particular ways the true reality of what they are communicating about, the inhabitants develop an intense desire to know the truth, and the eagerness with which they further investigate the subject then perfects their memory.

I spoke with them about this on another occasion as well; and since I knew they were communicating with the inhabitants of their own planet, I asked how they were teaching them. They said they do not tell the inhabitants how matters actually stand but only give them some inkling of it, so that their desire to explore and find out for themselves might be fed and increased. If instead they simply answered all the inhabitants' questions, that desire might die. They added that another reason they give misleading information is so that the truth can be seen more clearly, because every truth becomes more visible in relation to its opposite.

They have a custom of not telling anyone else what they know but nevertheless trying to find out from all others what the others know. Within their own community, though, they share everything, to the point that what one knows, all know, and what they all know each one knows.[1]   **36**

Since spirits from Mercury have an abundance of knowledge, they have a particular kind of pride as well. They think they know so much that there is hardly anything more to know. Some spirits from our planet told them, though, that what they know is not a lot but a little, and what they do not know is infinite in comparison. They said that what the spirits from Mercury know is like a trickle from a little spring, and what they do not know is like a vast ocean. They added that the first threshold of wisdom is to know, admit, and perceive that what they know is hardly anything at all in comparison to what they do not know.   **37**

To teach them that this was so, an angelic spirit was allowed to talk with them and review with them in general terms what they knew and what they did not know, showing that what they did not know was infinite, and that to all eternity they would be unable to comprehend even a general outline of the underlying reality. This spirit communicated using angelic images, communicating far more quickly than they were able to,

---

1. See note e on §15.

and since he was disclosing what they knew and what they did not know, they were stunned.

Later I saw an angel talking with them. He appeared somewhat above and on the right. He was from our planet. He listed a great many things they did not know, and then communicated with them using changes of state, which they said they did not understand at all. He told them that each change of state contained infinite details, and that each detail contained an infinity as well.

Because they had placed such pride in what they knew, when they heard this they began to feel profoundly humble. Their feelings of humility were represented by a lowering of their scroll (as a group they now began to look from a distance like a scroll, in front of me and off to the left, on a level below the navel). The scroll then appeared low in the middle but raised at each end and had a noticeable back-and-forth motion as well. They were told what this meant; namely, it was a reflection of what they were thinking as they were feeling humble; and it meant that the spirits who appeared at the raised ends were not yet feeling any humility. Then I saw the scroll split apart and the spirits who were not feeling humble were sent back toward their own planet, while the rest stayed where they were.

38 Some spirits from Mercury approached a man from our planet who had been especially celebrated for his learning during his earthly life (it was Christian Wolff). They were eager to have him tell them about a variety of subjects, but they became aware that what he was saying was not at all elevated above the sensory level of the earthly self. This was because when he was talking he was thinking about his own reputation, and tried to force things into various series just as he had in the world (we all stay very much ourselves in the other life). Then he wanted to go on and do the same with these series and keep drawing conclusions so as to form chains of a great many things that the spirits from Mercury did not see or acknowledge as true. This meant, they said, that the chains were not consistent with themselves or with the conclusions he drew from them, so they called them "the obscurity of authority." They stopped asking him substantive questions and inquired only what term he used for this and what term he used for that; but because the ideas he expressed in response were all matter-based and not spiritual in the least, they left him. In the other life we all speak spiritually, or communicate using spiritual images, if we believed in God in this world; and we speak materialistically if we did not believe.

[2] Let me take this opportunity to tell how things work out in the other life for scholars. On the one hand I wish to say how it is for those scholars who gain understanding through their own reflections and are motivated by a love of knowing what is true for its own sake and therefore for some purpose beyond worldly considerations. On the other hand I wish to say how it is for the scholars who base their work on what others have done without reflecting on it for themselves. This latter practice is typical of people who want to know what is true solely for the sake of their own reputation as scholars, to get from it respect or wealth in this world; and therefore for no purpose beyond worldly considerations. Let me insert one particular experience along these lines.

I became aware of a sound spreading from below, at my left side, and up toward my left ear. I could tell that some spirits were trying to get out of that region, but I could not tell what kind they were. When they did finally get out, they talked with me, saying they had been experts in logic and metaphysics, and that their thinking had been totally absorbed in such matters, but solely for the purpose of sounding erudite and thereby gaining status and wealth. They complained that now their lives were wretched because that had been their only reason for learning, which meant that their learning had not served to develop their reasoning faculties. Their speech was mumbling and slow.

[3] All the while, there were two spirits talking with each other above my head. When I asked who they were I was told that one of them had been one of the most famous minds on earth, and I was given to believe that it was Aristotle. I was not told who the second spirit was. The first spirit was then returned to the state he had been in during his life in the world (we can all be quite readily returned to the state we were in during our life in the world, because we bring our whole state of life with us). To my surprise, he came over to my *right* ear and started talking to me; his voice was hoarse, but what he was saying was sound. From the meaning of what he said I could perceive that his nature was completely different from that of the Scholastics whom I had seen coming up first. His own thoughts had been the source of his writings, and from them he had produced his philosophy. Therefore the terms he had come up with and had applied to the subjects he was thinking about were expressions for conveying ideas that had real depth. I realized also that what had taken him in that direction was a true feeling of delight and a genuine desire to know what was involved in thinking and understanding, and that he had followed faithfully the dictates of his spirit. That was why it was my right ear that he approached,

unlike his followers (the ones called Scholastics). The Scholastics did not go from thought to terms but from terms to thoughts, which is moving in the wrong direction. Many of them did not even get to thoughts, but simply stayed focused on terms; and the use they made of those terms was only to confirm whatever they chose and to superimpose an appearance of truth on things that were false in accordance with their zeal to persuade others. For them, then, philosophy was a means of going insane rather than becoming wise, and brought them darkness instead of light.

[4] I then talked with Aristotle about the science of reasoning. I said that what a young child spontaneously utters over the course of half an hour follows more rules of philosophy, reasoning, and logic than Aristotle himself could set forth in an entire volume, because there are components within every aspect of human thought and language, and the laws that govern these components come from the spiritual world. People who instead use an artificial system based on special terminology as a method of trying to achieve thought are rather like a dancer who wants to learn to dance by studying motor fibers and muscles: anyone whose mind is focused on this during an exercise can scarcely lift a foot. But dancers with none of this knowledge can move all the motor fibers spread over the whole body, coordinating the movement of the lungs, diaphragm, sides, arms, neck, and the rest—even though volumes would not suffice to describe what is going on anatomically. Much the same issue applies to people who with great effort base their thinking on terminology.

Aristotle agreed with this and said that if that is the way we are taught to think, we have the whole process upside down. He added that if someone actually wanted to become stupid, that was the correct way to proceed. If not, though, people ought to keep constantly in mind what is useful, and start their thinking from what lies within.

[5] He then showed me how he had viewed the Supreme Deity: he had envisioned the Deity as having a human face and a head encircled with rays of light. He said that he now knew that that divine-human being is the Lord and that the ring of light-rays depicts the divine emanation that comes from him and flows not only into heaven but into the physical universe, managing and governing them both. He added that to manage and govern heaven is to manage and govern the universe, because the two cannot be separated from each other. He also said that he had believed there was only one God, but God's various attributes and qualities had been given names that others eventually worshiped as separate gods.

[6] At that time I saw a vision of a woman who was reaching out her hand and trying to caress my cheek. When I wondered out loud about this, he said that while he was living in the world he often saw a woman like that who would almost caress his cheek and that her hand was beautiful. Angelic spirits [who were present] said that the ancients in general sometimes had visions of women like this and called them Pallases. They said that these visions had been given to Aristotle by a group of spirits who during their lives in the world, in even more ancient times, had taken delight in concepts and spent much time in thought, but lacked a philosophical system. Because spirits of this kind had been with Aristotle and had been delighted that he was thinking so deeply, they had represented to him an image of a woman like this.

[7] Lastly, he let me know the concept of the human soul or spirit he had formerly held, which at that time he referred to as the *pneuma*—that is to say, he had understood it as an unseen vital force, like something made of ether. He also said that he had known his spirit was going to live on after death, since it was his inner essence, and that essence is not subject to death, because it possesses the power of thought. Beyond that, however, the concepts he had formed concerning the soul were more vague than clear, because everything he had known about it he had come to on his own; very little had come from other ancients.

Aristotle himself is one of the sane spirits in the other life; many of his followers, though, are among the foolish.

On one occasion I saw some spirits from our planet in the company of spirits from Mercury and heard them talking with each other. One of the questions our spirits asked the spirits from Mercury was, "Whom do you believe in?" The spirits from Mercury replied that they believed in God; but when they were asked further questions about the God they believed in, they were unwilling to respond. This was because of their custom of not giving direct answers to questions.

Then the spirits from Mercury asked the spirits from our planet, "Whom do *you* believe in?" Our spirits said they believed in the Lord God. The spirits from Mercury, though, said they could tell that the spirits from our planet had no belief in God at all, but were in the habit of *saying* that they believed when in fact they did not. (Spirits from Mercury are extremely perceptive because they are constantly exercising their powers of perception in order to find out what others know.) These spirits from our planet were of the kind that, during their lives in the world, had confessed faith because the church had taught them to, but had not lived a life of faith; and people who do not live a life of faith [in this world] have no faith after death, because faith never becomes a part of them.ᵐ When the spirits from our planet heard this they became silent, because an awareness they were then granted made them recognize that it was true.

40   Some spirits were told by a heavenly source that spirits from the planet Mercury had at one time been promised that they would see the Lord. So the spirits around me asked the spirits from Mercury whether they remembered receiving this promise. They said they did remember receiving it, but they were not sure the promise had been so definite that there was no possibility of doubt about it.

While this conversation was going on, the sun of heaven appeared to them. (Only the inhabitants of the inmost or third heaven see the sun of heaven, which is the Lord—the rest just see its light.) When the spirits from Mercury saw the sun, however, they said that it was not the Lord God, because they did not see a face. Then the spirits had a conversation with each other, but I did not hear what they were saying.

Then, suddenly, the sun reappeared, but this time at its center was the Lord surrounded by a solar ring. When they saw this, the spirits from Mercury felt profoundly humbled and bowed themselves down.

At that time, the Lord appeared in the sun to spirits from our planet as well, those who had seen him in the flesh when he was on earth. One after another, a large number testified that this was the Lord, and they said this in front of everyone.

At the same time the Lord also appeared in the sun to spirits from the planet Jupiter, who said in the clearest terms that this was the one they had seen on their planet when the God of the universe had appeared to them.ⁿ

---

m. People who confess faith because they are taught to do so, but do not live a life of faith, do not actually have any faith: 3865, 7766, 7778, 7790, 7950, 8094. In fact, their deeper natures are opposed to the truths that belong to religious faith, even though during their lives in the world they do not realize this: 7790, 7950.

n. The Lord is the sun of heaven, the source of all the light that is there: 1053, 3636, 4060. The Lord appears as a sun to the people in his heavenly kingdom, where love for the Lord reigns supreme: 1521, 1529, 1530, 1531, 1837, 4696. He is seen at a middle altitude above the level of the right eye: 4321, 7078. In the Word, therefore, the sun means the Lord's divine love: 2495, 4060, 7083. The sun of our world is not visible to spirits or angels. In its place there is a kind of darkness behind them, in the direction that is opposite the sun of heaven or the Lord: 9755.

After they had seen the Lord some spirits were led forward and to **41** the right, and as they went they said that they were seeing a much clearer and purer light than they had ever seen before and that there could be no greater light—and at the time, it was evening here. There were a lot of people saying this.º

It is important to know that the sun of our world and the light that **42** comes from it are not in any way visible to any spirit. The light of our sun is like dense darkness to spirits and angels. Our sun remains in the consciousness of spirits only as a result of what they had seen when they were in the world and is presented to them as an image of something dark, at a considerable distance behind them, a little above the level of the head.

The planets in our solar system are seen by them in fixed positions with reference to the sun: Mercury appears behind and a little to the right; Venus appears to the left and a little behind; Mars appears out in front to the left; Jupiter too appears out in front and to the left, but farther away; Saturn appears straight ahead at a considerable distance; and our moon appears fairly high up to the left. The satellites of other planets, too, appear to the left of their planet. That is how the locations of the planets appear in the conceptions of the angels and spirits [from our earth]. The spirits from a given planet appear near their planet but outside it.

As for the spirits from Mercury in specific, though, they do not appear in one particular region or at one particular distance, but are sometimes in front, sometimes to the left, sometimes a little toward the back. This is because they are allowed to roam around the universe acquiring knowledge.

Some spirits from Mercury once appeared to me in the form of a **43** sphere to my left, and then in the shape of a scroll stretching far into the distance. I wondered where they were headed, for our planet or for some other. I soon noticed that they curved back and toward the right, and that their scroll unrolled as they were nearing the front region of the planet Venus. When they got there, though, they said that they did not

---

o. There is great light in the heavens, many levels above the light of midday on earth: 1117, 1521, 1532, 1619–1632, 4527, 5400, 8644. All the light in the heavens comes from the Lord as their sun: 1053, 1521, 3195, 3341, 3636, 3643, 4415, 9548, 9684, 10809. The divine truth that emanates from the divine goodness of the Lord's divine love appears in the heavens as light and is the source of all the light there: 3195, 3222, 5400, 8644, 9399, 9548, 9684. Heaven's light enlightens both the eyesight and the understanding that angels have: 2776, 3138. Heaven is said to have abundant light and warmth, which means that it has abundant wisdom and love: 3643, 9399, 9400.

want to remain in that place because the people there were evil; so they curved around to the back part of the planet and said that that was a place they wanted to stay because the people who lived there were good.

While this was going on, I felt a distinct change in my brain and strong activity within it as a result.

This led me to conclude that the spirits from that part of the planet Venus were in harmony with the spirits from Mercury. I gathered that those spirits from Venus related to a type of memory of matter-based concepts that harmonizes with the memory of non-matter-based concepts to which the spirits from Mercury relate. This is why I felt stronger activity from the spirits of Mercury when they were there.

44   I wanted to know what the faces and bodies of the inhabitants of the planet Mercury looked like—whether they looked like ours. A woman was then presented before my eyes who looked similar in every way to the women of our planet. She had a beautiful face, though it was smaller than the faces of women of our planet; she was about the same height, but her body was more slender. Her head was covered with a piece of linen arranged rather casually but becomingly. I was also shown a man. He too was more slender than men from our planet. He was wearing a dark blue garment, very close-fitting, with no folds or protrusions anywhere. I was told that this was what the men of that planet looked like and how they dressed.

I was then shown what the bulls and cows of their cattle looked like, which in fact were not all that different from those of our planet—smaller, though, and somewhat close in appearance to does and bucks.

45   I also asked them what the sun of our solar system looked like from their planet. They said that it looked huge, larger than it does when seen from other planets. They said they had learned of this contrast from seeing the mental image of the Sun that the spirits from other planets had.

They went on to say that that their climate was moderate, not too hot or too cold. It occurred to them to add that the Lord saw to it that their planet should not be too hot for them even though it was nearer the Sun than others, since the heat we feel depends not on our proximity to the Sun but on the depth and therefore the density of the atmosphere where we are, as we can see from the coolness felt on high mountains even in places where the climate at lower altitudes is hot. There is also the fact that the temperature varies with the angle of incidence of the Sun's rays, as we can see from the seasons of summer and winter that each region goes through.

This is what it has been granted to me to know about the spirits and inhabitants of the planet Mercury.

The Planet *Jupiter* and Its Spirits and Inhabitants

I have been allowed to interact with the spirits and angels from Jupiter **46** over a longer period than with spirits and angels from other planets, so I can report more about their state of life and the state of their planet's inhabitants. There have been a number of indications that this is where these spirits came from, and I have been told so by a heavenly source as well.

The actual planet Jupiter is in no way visible to spirits and angels because **47** there is no way for any planet to be visible to people in the spiritual world—only the spirits and angels who come from that planet are visible. The ones from the planet Jupiter can be seen toward the front on the left at a fair distance, and this location is constant (see §42 above). That is where spirits and angels visualize the planet as being, too. The spirits from each planet are near their planet because they were originally among that planet's inhabitants (since everyone becomes a spirit after death) and also because their character is similar to that of the inhabitants and therefore they can be with them and be of service to them.

They told me that in the region of the planet where they had lived **48** their earthly lives there were a great many people, as many as the land could feed. They said that the land was fertile and abundant in every way. In their world people desired no more than they needed for the necessities of life, and they saw no use in having more than that. That was why so great a population could be sustained there.

They said that their greatest concern was for the raising of their children and that they loved their children most tenderly.

They went on to tell me that the inhabitants were divided into peoples, extended families, and individual households, and that all of the **49** inhabitants lived separately like this, among their own. This meant that they spent most of their time with their relatives. Further, no one longed for anyone else's possessions. It never crossed anyone's mind to covet something that belonged to someone else, let alone to lay claim to it by some scheme, still less to break in and steal it. They regarded this as a crime against human nature—as something horrendous.

When I tried to tell them that in our world there are wars and robberies and murders, they turned away and did not want to hear it.

[2] Angels have told me that the earliest people on our planet lived like that. They too were divided into peoples, extended families, and households. All of them were content with what they had. Profiting at the expense of others and ruling over others out of self-love were utterly unknown to them. This was why ancient times on this earth and especially the earliest times were preferred by the Lord over later times. Since this was the prevalent state, innocence reigned supreme then, accompanied by wisdom. Everyone did what was good because it was good, and what was upright because it was upright. They knew nothing about doing things that were good and upright only for the sake of their own reputation or for profit. Back then people did not say anything unless it was true, and this was not so much because it was the truth as because doing so was good—that is, not just from their understanding by itself but from their will in conjunction with their understanding. That is what ancient times were like.

Because of this, angels were able to interact with people on earth in those days and lift people's minds almost entirely out of their bodily perspective into heaven. Angels were able to take people around heaven and show them grand and joyful things, sharing their own joys and happiness with them. These times were well known to ancient authors, who called them the Golden or Saturnian Age.

[3] The reason those times were like this was, as just noted, that the ancients lived divided into peoples. The peoples were divided into extended families, the extended families were divided into households, and each household lived as a separate unit. It never crossed anyone's mind to claim someone else's inheritance in order to gain wealth and power. Self-love and love for the world were then far away. People were just as happy when things went well for someone else as when they went well for themselves.

[4] As time went on, though, and a craving for power and excessive wealth invaded the mind, the situation reversed. Humankind then gathered into kingdoms and empires for the sake of safety; and since the laws of caring and conscience that had been written on the human heart became no longer operative, people needed to enact laws to constrain

violence, laws that used status and wealth as rewards and loss of status and wealth as punishments.

Because of this change in our state, heaven began moving farther and farther away from us; and this has continued to the present age, when people are no longer sure whether there is a heaven or a hell, and some even flatly deny that they exist.

I mention this to illustrate by parallelism what the state of people from Jupiter is like and why they have such integrity and wisdom, which will be described in what follows.

Spending a lot of time with spirits from Jupiter gradually made it **50** plain to me that they are more upright than the spirits of many other planets. Their quiet approach as they came to me, their presence, and the inflow from them that ensued, was so sweet and gentle that there are no words to describe it. In the other life, the character of all spirits is quite evident because there is an inflow from them that communicates their feelings. Uprightness comes across as gentleness and sweetness, gentleness because the upright fear doing harm, and sweetness because they love doing good. I could tell very clearly how the type of gentleness and sweetness flowing in from good spirits of our planet differed from the type flowing in from theirs.

They said that when some slight difference of opinion arises among them, they see a kind of thin white streak of light like a bolt of lightning, or else they see a narrow band of twinkling wandering stars; but the difficulties between them are soon resolved. Twinkling stars that wander mean something that is false, while twinkling stars that are fixed mean something that is true; so the wandering stars were a reflection of their disagreement.[a]

I could tell that spirits from Jupiter were present not only from the **51** sweetness and gentleness of their approach and of their inflow but also from the fact that they flowed particularly into my face, making it cheerful and smiling the whole time they were with me. They said that they had this effect on the faces of the inhabitants of their planet when they visited them, to inspire a sense of peace and delight in their hearts. They inspired me with peace and delight as well; I could feel it filling my chest and my heart.

---

a. Stars in the Word mean knowledge of what is good and true and therefore truths themselves: 2495, 2849, 4697. In the other life truths are represented by stars that are fixed and falsities are represented by stars that wander: 1128.

It took away my cravings and my worries about the future, along with the restlessness and misery and emotional upheaval those feelings cause.

This made it possible for me to see what life was like for the inhabitants of Jupiter. One can get to know the nature of a planet's inhabitants from the spirits from that planet because we all bring with us the life we led in the physical world and go on living that same kind of life when we become spirits.

I became aware that their state was one of blessedness, meaning profound inner happiness. I observed this because I was able to tell that their deeper levels were not closed off but were open toward heaven. The more open our deeper levels are toward heaven, the more open we are to receiving divine goodness; and blessedness and profound happiness come with that goodness. It is totally different for people who are not living within the design of heaven; their deeper levels are closed, and their outer levels are open to this world.

52 I was shown what the faces of the inhabitants of Jupiter look like. I did not actually see inhabitants themselves, but I saw spirits whose faces were like the ones they had had when they lived on their planet. Before I saw them, though, one of their angels appeared behind a bright cloud and gave permission. I was then shown two faces. They were glowing and beautiful like the faces of people of our own planet. Honesty and modesty radiated from them.

[2] When spirits from Jupiter were with me, the faces of people from our planet looked smaller than usual to me. This was because what was flowing in from the spirits was a concept they had that their own faces were larger. The people who live on that planet have the belief that after they die their faces will become larger and rounder. Since this concept makes a deep impression on them it persists in them after death; and when they become spirits, they see themselves as having larger faces.

[3] The reason the inhabitants of Jupiter believe their faces will be larger after death is, as they say, that the face is not part of the body, since they see, hear, speak, and express their thoughts through their faces, and since in this manner the mind can be seen through the face. So their concept of the face is that it is an outward form of the mind, and since they know that they will become wiser after their life in the physical world, they believe that their face, as an outward form of their mind, will become larger.

[4] They also believe that after death they will sense a fire that will warm their faces from within. They get this notion because the wiser of

them know that, spiritually understood, fire means love, that love is the fire of life, and that for angels this fire is the source itself of their life.[b] If they have led lives devoted to heavenly love their dream comes true [after death] and they feel their face grow warm and the deeper levels of their mind catch fire with love.

[5] Because of this, the inhabitants of that planet frequently wash and cleanse their faces and carefully protect them from the heat of the sun. They have a bluish covering made from the bark or cork of a tree that they put around their heads to shield their faces.

[6] Through my eyes they have seen the faces of people of our planet.[c] They said that these did not look good, and that any beauty they had was on the surface of the skin, not in the fibers within. They were astounded that some of the faces they saw had warts or pimples or were deformed in other ways; they said that they had never seen things like that among their own people. Some faces made them smile, though. These were the ones that were cheerful and smiling and also those that protruded a bit around the lips.

The reason they responded with a smile to faces with lips that protrude is that most of their communication takes place by means of the face and especially the region around the lips. It is also because they never pretend—that is, say something other than what they are thinking—so they exert no control over their faces but let them freely reflect what is within.

It is different for people who have learned to dissimulate from childhood on. This makes them control their faces interiorly to prevent any of their thinking from showing through. Exteriorly their faces are not free either, but must be prepared to relax or else to constrict depending on what seems shrewdest.

An examination of the [nerve and muscle] fibers and surrounding tissues of the lips will support the truth of this point: There we find intricate

---

b. In the Word, fire means life in either sense, [good life or evil life]: 934, 4906, 5215. The sacred fire and the fire in heaven [mentioned in the Word] mean divine love and every desire that comes from that love: 934, 6314, 6832. Hellish fire means love for ourselves and for the world and every craving that comes from those loves: 934, 1861, 5071, 6314, 6832, 7575, 10747. Love is the fire of life; life itself actually comes from love: 4906, 5071, 6832.

c. Spirits and angels do not see things that are in our subsolar world on their own, but some have seen them through my eyes: 1880.

series of fibers interwoven and interconnected, created not only for eating and verbal speech but also for expressing the concepts in our minds.

54   I have been shown how their thoughts are expressed through their faces. The feelings they have, stemming from what they love, are displayed in their overall expression and the way it changes, while the thoughts within these feelings are displayed in variations in specific tissues beneath the surface, which are indescribable.

The inhabitants of the planet Jupiter also have verbal speech, but not as resonant as ours. Each of the two kinds of communication helps the other; their verbal speech is brought to life by their facial communication.

[2] I have been told by angels that on every planet the very first form of speech has been facial, using the two basic means of the lips and the eyes. The reason this kind of speech comes first is that the face has been formed to reflect what we think and what we want. That is why the face is called the image and index of the mind. It is also because honesty was a characteristic of the earliest or primal times. People did not have thoughts, and did not want to have thoughts, that they were unwilling to show in their faces. This allowed the feelings of their minds and their consequent thoughts to be vividly and fully presented in their faces. So their thoughts and feelings were visible to others' eyes in a single form containing many details at once. This kind of speech therefore surpassed verbal speech the way seeing something surpasses hearing about it—for example, seeing a field for yourself as opposed to hearing and understanding a verbal description of it.

They added that this kind of speech was compatible with the speech of angels; it allowed the people of those times to be in actual communication with angels. In fact, when our face speaks or our mind speaks through our face, that is angelic speech in its outermost earthly form. This is not the case when our mouth is communicating verbally.

As should be clear to everyone, the earliest people could not have had verbal speech, because the words of a language are not instilled directly but must be invented and associated with things, something that can happen only with the passage of time.[d]

---

d. The earliest people on this planet communicated by means of their faces and lips through internal breathing: 607, 1118, 7361. The inhabitants of some other planets, too, use a similar way of communicating: 4799, 7359, 8248, 10587. How excellent and perfect that form of communication is: 7360, 10587, 10708.

[3] For as long as honesty and straightforwardness prevailed among people this kind of communication continued; but as soon as the mind began to think one thing and say another (which happened when we began to love ourselves and not our neighbor) verbal speech began to gain ground, and the face became either silent or deceptive.

This brought about a change in the inner form of the face, a contraction and hardening, and it became almost devoid of life, although it still looked to others as though it was alive because self-love was burning within it. That underlying absence of life is not visible to our eyes. It is, however, visible to the eyes of angels, since they see what lies within. So this is the nature of the faces of people who think one thing and say another; this is the effect of the pretense, hypocrisy, guile, and deceit that constitute prudence nowadays.

Things are different in the other life, though. There we are not allowed to say one thing and think another. Any inconsistency is in fact perceived with utmost clarity in every word; and when it is perceived, spirits guilty of the inconsistency are ejected from the interaction and punished. Thereafter they are compelled by various means to speak in alignment with their thinking and to think in alignment with their willing until eventually they have a unified mind and not a divided one. If they are good, then, they intend what is good and think and say the truth that stems from that goodness; if they are evil they intend what is evil and think and say the falsity that stems from that evil. Until this happens, the good are not raised into heaven and the evil are not cast into hell. The purpose of all this is that in hell there should be nothing but what is evil and the falsity that stems from it, and that in heaven there should be nothing but what is good and the truth that stems from it.

I have also been told a number of other things about the inhabitants of that planet by spirits from there—about how they walk, for example, about their food, and about their homes.

55

As to how they walk, they do not walk upright like the inhabitants of our planet and of many others, nor do they go on all fours like animals, but help themselves along with their hands, from time to time straightening themselves up on their feet partway. Every third step as they go along, they look to the side and back, twisting their body a little, in a single, quick motion. This is because it is considered impolite for them not to show their face to others.

[2] When they are walking like this they keep their faces raised much the way we do, in order to see the sky as well as the ground. They do

not keep their faces down and look only at the ground—this they call damnable. The worthless among them, though, do in fact do this; and if these do not develop a habit of raising their faces, they are exiled from their community.

[3] When they sit, they look like the people of our planet with respect to their upper bodies, which are upright, but not with respect to their legs, which are crossed. As when walking, so also when they are sitting they take care not to be seen from behind, only face to face. They want others to see their face because their face reveals their mind. They never do, and never could, put on a face that is at odds with their mind. This means that the people present with them know quite clearly what their attitude toward them is. They do not hide it. This applies especially to knowing whether the friendliness being shown is genuine or forced.

This was demonstrated for me by Jupiter's spirits and confirmed by its angels. This, furthermore, explains why its spirits seem not to walk upright like others but to proceed almost like swimmers, helping themselves along with their hands, and looking around from time to time.

56   The ones who live in the tropical regions of that planet go naked except for a loincloth. They are not embarrassed by nudity, since their minds are chaste. They love only their spouses, and loathe acts of adultery. They were very surprised that when spirits from our planet hear that they walk like that and go naked, the spirits from our planet snicker and think lewd thoughts, giving no attention to their heavenly way of life but only to that sort of thing. The spirits from Jupiter said this was an indication that we are concerned more with bodily and worldly things than with heavenly ones and that our minds are obsessed with filthy thoughts. The spirits from Earth were told that nudity is neither shameful nor scandalous to people who lead lives that are chaste and innocent, though it is both of these things to people who lead lives that are lewd and sexually unclean.

57   When the inhabitants of that planet lie down in their beds they turn their face inward, toward the center of the room, rather than outward, toward the wall. Their spirits told me this and explained the reason. They do this because they see it as turning their face toward the Lord; if they face the wall they see it as turning away from the Lord. The idea [that I should face away from the wall] had occurred to me at times when I was in bed, but before this conversation I had no idea why.

58   They enjoy taking their time at meals, not so much because they enjoy the food but because they enjoy the conversation that goes with it.

When they sit at table they do not sit on stools or benches or on raised grassy banks or on the grass but on the leaves from a particular tree. They were reluctant to say what kind of tree the leaves were from, but when I kept guessing and eventually mentioned fig leaves, they said yes.

They said further that they do not prepare their food to suit their taste, but primarily for its benefit; in any case, they said, to them any food that is beneficial tastes good.

[2] There was a discussion of this among some spirits, and they said that this is right and proper for people because it shows that they are at heart concerned to have a sound mind in a sound body. It is different for people for whom the taste of their food takes precedence. This approach makes the body sicken or at least weaken inwardly; and therefore the mind does too, since its functioning is affected by the inner condition of the parts of our body that receive our mind, just as our sight and hearing depend on the condition of our eyes and ears. Therefore it is a form of insanity to believe that all the joy in life is to be found in luxury and self-gratification. This attitude leads us to be skillful in matters that concern the body and the world but stupid in matters that require thought and judgment. This is the origin of the view that people are just like brute animals—and people who think this way even compare themselves to animals, not inappropriately.

I was also shown their homes. They are simple wooden structures, but paneled inside with light blue bark and dotted with little stars all around and overhead to resemble the sky. This is because they want to bring into their homes an image of the sky with its stars, since they believe the stars are the dwellings of angels. **59**

They also have tents, which are domed and oblong. These too are dotted with little stars on a blue background. The inhabitants gather there in the daytime to prevent their faces from being damaged by the heat of the sun. They take great care in assembling and cleaning these tents. These are also where they eat.

When spirits from Jupiter would see horses on our planet the horses looked unusually small to me, though they were perfectly strong and tall. This was because of the image these spirits had of their own planet's horses. They said that they had horses that were similar but much larger. The horses on their planet were wild and roamed the forests, and when the inhabitants saw them they were terrified even though the horses did them no harm. They added that this fear was natural or instinctive for them. This made me ponder the cause of their fear. Spiritually understood, a **60** horse means an intellect shaped by factual information;[e] therefore because they dread cultivating their intellect with worldly information this fear of horses flows into them.

As we will see below [§62], they have no interest in information generated by human learning.

61 Spirits of that planet do not want to be in the company of spirits from our planet because they are different in temperament and custom. They say that spirits from our planet are crafty, and quick and clever at evil schemes, but do not know much about what is good or give it much thought.

Spirits from Jupiter are much wiser than spirits from our planet. They describe us as talking a lot and thinking very little and therefore having almost no inner perception or ability even to tell what is good. This leads them to conclude that the people of our planet are external by nature.

[2] On one occasion some evil spirits from our planet were allowed to exercise their evil skills and harass some spirits from Jupiter who were with me. The spirits from Jupiter stood this for quite a while, but eventually said they could no longer endure it. They came to believe there could not be anyone worse than these spirits, because the spirits twisted their imagination and thinking so much that they felt shackled and could not be rescued and freed except by divine intervention.

When I read them passages from the Word about our Savior's suffering on the cross, some European spirits put up horrifying roadblocks in order to steer the spirits from Jupiter away from belief. I asked who these European spirits were and what they had done in the world. I discovered that some of them had been preachers and many had been Jesuits, that is, members of the Society of the Lord. I told the spirits from Jupiter that during their earthly lives these evil spirits had been able to move crowds to tears with their sermons about the Lord's suffering. I added that they had been able to do this because in the world their thinking had been very different from what they said, so their hearts had one agenda but their mouths presented something else. Now, though, they were not allowed to speak deceptively, because when they became spirits they were forced to say exactly what they thought.

---

e. A horse means our intellectual ability: 2760, 2761, 2762, 3217, 5321, 6125, 6400, 6534, 7024, 8146, 8148. The white horse in the Book of Revelation means an understanding of the Word: 2760.

The spirits from Jupiter were absolutely stunned that there could be such a discrepancy between the inside and the outside of anyone, that is, that anyone could say one thing but think something completely different. For them this would be impossible.

[3] They were astonished, then, to hear that many people from our planet actually become angels and are totally different from these people at heart; they had presumed that all the people on our planet were alike. It was explained to them that many were not like the ones they had met. There are people who think with good intent and not with evil intent like those others, and the ones with good intent become angels.

To show them that this was true, choruses of angels from our planet, one after another, came to them from heaven, joining with one voice and with one accord in praise to the Lord.[f] The choruses gave the spirits of Jupiter who were with me such pleasure that they seemed to themselves to have been caught up into heaven. The choruses' praises went on for about an hour. I could feel the delight the spirits took in these praises because it was communicated to me. The spirits said they would describe this experience to their companions who were elsewhere.

Wisdom, for the inhabitants of Jupiter, is thinking well and fairly about the situations they encounter in the course of their lives. From early childhood on they eagerly learn this kind of wisdom from their parents and pass it on to the next generation, and since they love it because it belonged to their parents, it grows. **62**

They know nothing whatever of the kinds of academic knowledge we have on our planet and have no desire to know them. They call them "shadows" and liken them to clouds between us and the sun. They got this negative impression of academic knowledge from some spirits from our planet who bragged to them about the wisdom they had developed from book learning.

[2] These boasting spirits from our planet were people who had equated wisdom with nothing more than the contents of memory—for example, languages they knew, and in particular Hebrew, Greek, and Latin; accounts of events familiar to the world of the well-read; critical reviews; mere experiments; terminology (especially philosophical terminology); and other such

---

f. It is called a chorus when a number of spirits speak at the same time and are of one mind: 2595, 2596, 3350 (which include descriptions). They speak with one accord: 1648, 1649 (which include descriptions). In the other life, choruses serve to bring people into a state of unanimity: 5182.

things—all without using these as means to wisdom, because they equated the information itself with wisdom. Since they had not used their learning to cultivate their rational ability, in the other life they have very little perceptiveness. Because their [mental] vision is restricted to terminology and is based on it, the information they have is like dust to people of this sort, or like clouds in front of their intellectual sight (see §38 above). The ones who had become proud as a result of their learning are even less perceptive. Further, the ones who had used academic learning to undermine and destroy the teachings of the church and of faith had utterly destroyed their own intellects. Like owls, they see in darkness [rather than light]; they see falsity as true and evil as good.

[3] On the basis of their conversations with people like this, the spirits from Jupiter drew the conclusion that academic learning causes obscurity and [mental] blindness. However, they were told that on our planet academic study is a means to opening an intellectual sight that makes it possible to see things in the light of heaven. Nevertheless, because things that concern nothing more than earthly and sensory life have become predominant here, academic pursuits have become a means to insanity, that is, a means of convincing ourselves to believe in nature rather than the Divine and in this world rather than heaven. [4] They were also told that in and of itself academic learning is spiritual wealth and that people who possess it are like people who possess worldly wealth. In both cases the wealth can be of benefit to themselves, their neighbor, and their country, but can also be used to do harm. This learning is also like clothing, which can be useful and attractive, but can also be a source of pride for people who want to be respected simply because of the way they dress.

The spirits from Jupiter understood this well, but it still puzzled them that during life in the physical world these people stayed with the means, attaching more importance to the building blocks of wisdom than to wisdom itself, not seeing that immersing their minds in these concerns and failing to raise them any higher was causing them darkness and blindness.

63 A spirit came up to me from the lower earth and said that he had heard what I was talking about with some other spirits but did not understand anything we were saying about a spiritual life and its light. When he was asked whether he wanted to learn, he said that he had not come with that in mind. This led me to the conclusion that he would not be able to grasp such matters; he was extremely stupid. I was told by some angels, though, that when he was living in the world he had been one of the more celebrated scholars. He was cold, as we could definitely tell from his breath. This was a sign that the light within him was merely earthly and not spiritual. So by his learning he had not opened the path to heaven's light but had closed it instead.

Since the inhabitants of the planet Jupiter gain intelligence by a different route than that followed by the inhabitants of our planet and since they are also of a different basic disposition because of the way they live, they cannot be with us very long. They either leave us or send us away. **64**

There are auras, properly called spiritual auras, that constantly radiate from every spirit, that in fact flow out in waves. These auras originate in the activity of the spirits' feelings and associated thoughts and therefore the life within them.g In the other life, auras are always what determine whether people associate with each other. Auras that are in harmony join people together in response to the degree of their harmony, and auras that conflict repel people from each other in response to the degree of their discord.

[2] In the universal human, spirits and angels who come from Jupiter have to do with the *image-making activity of thought* and therefore inner creativity, while spirits from our planet have to do with various functions of the outer parts of the body. When these latter functions are trying to be in control, the creative or image-making activity of thought cannot flow into them from within. As a result, there is a conflict between the auras arising from the way each group lives.

As for their worship of God, it is all based on the acknowledgment of our Lord as the Highest, the one who rules heaven and earth. They call him "the Only Lord," and since they acknowledge and worship him during their physical lives they seek him and find him after death. This is the same Lord we worship. **65**

I asked them whether they know that the Only Lord is human. They have replied that they all know he is human because in their world many people have seen him as a human, who teaches them about truth, protects them, and gives them eternal life if they worship him by doing what is good.

They said further that he has revealed to them how they should live and what they should believe, and that what he has revealed to them has

---

g. Every human, spirit, and angel has an aura that flows out in waves from and envelops that individual; this is the spiritual or life aura: 4464, 5179, 7454. It flows out from their feelings and associated thoughts: 2489, 4464, 6206. In the other life, auras determine both the alliances and the divisions that occur: 6206, 9606, 9607, 10312.

been handed on from parents to children. A body of teaching flows from this to all their families and to a whole people who are descendants of the same ancestor.

They added that it seemed to them as though they had that body of teaching written on their minds. What makes them think this is that they perceive immediately and recognize seemingly instinctively whether what others are saying about heaven's life within humankind is true or not.

[2] They did not know that their Only Lord was born as a human on our planet; but they said that knowing this does not matter to them—only that he alone is human and governs the universe. When I said that on our planet he is called Christ Jesus, "Christ" meaning "Anointed One" or "King" and "Jesus" meaning "Savior," they said that they do not worship him as their King, because the notion of kingship feels too worldly to them, but that they do worship him as their Savior.

When some spirits from our planet challenged the idea that their Only Lord was the same as our Lord, the spirits from Jupiter removed all doubt by recalling that they had seen him in the sun [of the spiritual world] and had recognized him as the one they had seen on their planet (see §40 above). [3] On one [earlier] occasion some doubt suddenly flowed into some spirits from Jupiter who were with me, doubt as to whether their Only Lord was the same as our Lord; but this doubt that flowed in for a moment was also dispelled in a moment. It was flowing in from some spirits from our planet. Then (which surprised me) the spirits felt such shame at having doubted this for even a moment that they blushed and asked me not to tell anyone, so that they would not be accused of any disbelief when in fact they knew this better than anyone else.

[4] These spirits were deeply moved and delighted to hear it said that their Only Lord is in fact the only human and that all people are referred to as human only because of what comes from him. We are human to the extent that we are images of him, that is, to the extent that we love him and love our neighbor, and therefore to the extent that we are devoted to doing what is good, since good that is done out of love and faith *is* the image of the Lord.

66 Once when I was reading in the seventeenth chapter of John about the Lord's love and about his glorification there were some spirits from Jupiter with me. When they heard what it said, they were filled with a sense of holiness and declared that all these things were divine. Then, though, some spirits from our planet who were unbelievers repeatedly set up obstacles [to a belief in the Lord's divinity], saying that he was born as a baby, lived a human life, looked like any other human, was crucified, and more along the same lines. The spirits from Jupiter paid no attention to this, though. They said that their own devils were similar and that they loathed them. They added that there was absolutely nothing heavenly dwelling in the minds of these spirits, only a worldliness that they referred to as "slag." They said they could also tell that this was the case from the fact that when these spirits heard that people walked around naked on Jupiter, lewdness immediately took control of their thoughts, and that they gave no thought to the heavenly way of life [practiced by people on Jupiter] even though they had heard about that as well.

I was able to determine how clear the perception of things spiritual is in spirits from Jupiter from seeing how they portrayed the way the Lord changes immoral desires into good ones. They represented the intellectual mind as a beautiful form and portrayed the living force of desire as a motion that was shaped to fit that form. There are no words to describe how they did this—so skillfully that angels joined in praising them. **67**

Some scholars from our planet were also present at the time, scholars who had immersed their minds in the terminology of the academic disciplines, and had written and thought a great deal about form, substance, the material and the immaterial, and the like, but had not put any of this information to use. They could not understand this representation at all.

On Jupiter they take the greatest possible care to prevent anyone from slipping into warped opinions about the Only Lord; and if they notice that people are beginning to think dark thoughts about him they give them a warning, then deter them by threats and eventually by punishments. They said they have observed that if something like this creeps into a family, what is effective in removing the warped opinion from their midst is not other members of the community threatening them with death but spirits restricting [the offenders'] breathing and the life it gives them, after first threatening them on pain of death. This is because on their planet spirits talk with them and punish them if they have done or are intending to do something evil (more on this below [§72]). So if they are thinking evil thoughts about the Only Lord and do not repent, they are threatened with death. That is how the worship of the Lord is maintained there, since to them the Lord is the Supreme Deity. **68**

They said that they do not have days that are set aside as sacred, but that every morning at sunrise and every evening at sunset they hold holy worship of the Only Lord in their tents, and that they accompany these with their own unique music. **69**

70   Further, I was told that on that planet there are some people who call themselves holy ones and demand under threat of punishment that their servants—and they like to have an ever increasing number of them—call them "lords." They even prohibit their servants from worshiping the Lord of the universe, saying that they themselves are "mediating lords" and that any requests made to them will be forwarded to the Lord of the universe.

They do not call the Lord of the universe (who is our Lord) "the Only Lord," as everyone else does, but "the Highest Lord," since they call themselves "lords" as well.

[2] They call the sun of their world the face of the Highest Lord and believe he has his home there, so they worship the sun. The other inhabitants avoid them and do not want to interact with them, both because they worship the sun and because they call themselves "lords" and are worshiped as demigods by their servants.

[3] Some spirits showed me what they wear on their head—a tall, dark hat.

[4] In the other life, people like this can be seen on the left at some height; they sit there like idols and at first are worshiped by their former servants. Later, though, their servants ridicule them.

Remarkably, their faces glow there as if they were on fire, which happens because they had thought of themselves as holy ones. Yet even though their faces look fiery, they are cold and intensely desire to feel warmer. This shows that the fire that gives them their glow is the fire of self-love and is illusory.

In order to get warm they chop wood, and as they do, a human shape appears to them beneath the logs, which they try to chop up along with the logs. They have this experience because they attribute merit and holiness to themselves; and people who do this in the world seem to themselves in the other life to be chopping wood. As I have mentioned elsewhere [*Secrets of Heaven* 1110, 2784, 6393], some of the people from our planet have the same experience. By way of example, let me cite one such experience [*Secrets of Heaven* 4943].

> In the lower earth, under the soles of the feet, there are people who have placed merit in their own good deeds and actions. Many of them seem to themselves to be chopping wood. The place where they are is quite cold, and they seem to feel warmed up by their labor. I was talking with them, and it occurred to me to ask if they wished to leave that place. They said that they still had not done enough work to deserve it.

When that state is completed, though, they are released. These spirits are earthly in nature, because trying to earn salvation for ourselves is not spiritual, because it comes from our own selfhood and not from the Lord. They consider themselves to be better than others, and some of them even despise others. If in the other life they are not granted more joy than others they resent the Lord; so when they are chopping wood it seems as though there is something of the Lord underneath the logs. This comes from their resentment.[h]

It is quite common on that planet for spirits to talk with the inhab-   **71**
itants, to teach them, and also to punish them if they have done evil things. Their angels have told me many things about this, so I would like to lay out some of them here.

The reason spirits talk with the inhabitants there is that the inhabitants give a great deal of thought to heaven and life after death and are not as concerned with their life in the world. They know that they are going to continue living after they die and that they will be in a happy state in accord with the state of their inner self that has taken shape in the world.

In ancient times, on our planet too talking with spirits and angels was normal, for the same reason—because people then were thinking a lot about heaven and not much about the world; but that living communication with heaven was later closed off when we turned from being internal to being external, or (which is the same thing) began to give a great deal of thought to this world and little to heaven. This was even more the case when we no longer believed in the existence of heaven and hell or saw ourselves as essentially spirits who would go on living after death. In fact, nowadays people believe that the body has a life of its own and no longer think it is sustained by its spirit. So the only kind of resurrection they can believe in is that they will be resurrected in their bodies.

As for the presence of spirits with the inhabitants of Jupiter, there   **72**
are spirits who punish them, spirits who teach them, and spirits who govern them. The ones who punish them attach themselves to the inhabitants'

---

h. Only the Lord has merit and righteousness: 9715, 9975, 9979, 9981, 9982. People who place merit in their deeds, that is, who want to earn heaven through the good things they have done, want to be waited on in the other life and are never satisfied: 6393. They despise their neighbors, and are angry against the Lord himself if they do not get their reward: 9976. What their portion in the other life is like: 942, 1774, 1877, 2027. They are among those in the lower earth who seem to themselves to be chopping wood: 1110, 4943.

left sides and then lean toward their backs; and once they are in position they draw from their subjects' memory everything the subjects have thought and done. This is easy for spirits because when they approach people they enter everything in their memory.[i]

If they discover that people have done evil things or have had evil thoughts they criticize them; and they punish them, too, with pains in their joints, feet, or hands, or pain in the general area of their abdomen. This is also something spirits can do very skillfully when it is permitted. When spirits of this kind are approaching people they cause a trembling accompanied by fear; this lets people know they are coming. Evil spirits can strike people with fear when they approach, especially spirits who were robbers during their lives in the physical world.

[2] To teach me what these spirits do when they come to someone from their planet, a spirit of this sort was allowed to come to me. As he approached, I was filled with a palpable fear and trembling. I was not trembling inwardly, though, but outwardly, since I knew that it was this kind of spirit. I was able to see him as well, and he looked like a dark cloud with wandering stars in it. Stars that wander mean falsities, and stars that are fixed mean truths.[j] He attached himself to my left side toward the back and began to criticize me for things I had done and thought, things he was drawing out of my memory, and began to put a dark interpretation on them, but was held back by angels. When he realized that he was with someone who was not from his own planet he started a conversation with me, and said that when he came to people, he knew absolutely everything they had done and thought. He added that he criticized them severely and also punished them with various kinds of pain.

[3] On another occasion a punitive spirit of this sort came to me and attached himself to my left side below the waist. Like the earlier one, he tried to punish me, but he too was held back by angels. Still, he showed me the kinds of punishment he was allowed to inflict on the people of his planet if they had done or were intending to do evil things. In addition to pains in the joints, he also caused a painful restriction of the middle of the abdomen that felt like a sharp-edged belt being cinched too tight. Then on and off again he made it hard to breathe, causing them distress. In addition, he would prevent them from being able to eat anything other

---

i. See note b on §11.

j. See note a on §50.

than bread for some period of time. Finally he would threaten them with death if they did not stop doing evil, and with the accompanying loss of all their joy in their spouses, children, and friends, the pain of which he was able to make them feel at the time of the threat.

The spirits who teach the inhabitants also attach themselves to the left side, but more toward the front. They criticize people, too, but mildly, and soon move on to teaching them how they should live. They also look dark, though not like clouds as the earlier ones did—rather, they seem to be wearing sackcloth. [2] They are called teachers, while the former ones are called punitive spirits.

When these spirits are present, angelic spirits are present as well who station themselves by the inhabitant's head and fill it with their own unique influence. Their presence there is perceived as a gentle breathing, since they fear that the inhabitant might otherwise feel some pain or anxiety, if only a small amount, at their approach and inflow. They govern both the punitive spirits and the teaching spirits, and make sure that the punitive spirits do nothing worse to the person than the Lord permits and that the teaching spirits only say things that are true.

When a punitive spirit was with me there were also some angelic spirits [from Jupiter] with me who kept my face constantly cheerful and smiling, the region around my lips protruding, and my mouth slightly open. When they have the Lord's permission, angels can easily flow in and do this. They said that they cause this kind of expression on the inhabitants of their planet when they are present with them.

If, after having been punished and instructed, the inhabitants again either do evil or plan to do it and do not restrain themselves in accord with the principles of truth, the spirit returns and punishes them more severely. Still, the angelic spirits temper the punishment to fit the intent behind those actions and the will behind those plans.

We can tell from this that the angels from Jupiter who are stationed by their inhabitants' heads are carrying out a kind of judgment on the inhabitants, because they flow in and allow some things, temper others, and prevent still others. I was told, though, that they themselves are not the ones passing judgment. Only the Lord is the true Judge, and every instruction the angels give the punitive and teaching spirits is something that in actuality they have received from the Lord; the judgments they make merely appear to come from themselves.

While the spirits there are able to talk to people, the people are not allowed to talk back to the spirits except to say, once they have been instructed, "We won't do that anymore." They are not allowed to tell any-one what the spirits who were with them said, either. If they do, they are punished afterward.

At first, the spirits from Jupiter who were with me thought that they were talking with someone from their own planet; but when I responded to them and even said I was thinking of publishing and thus communi-cating to others things like this, and told them they would not be allowed to punish or instruct me, they realized that they were not with someone from their planet.

76 When they are with someone there are two signs that appear to those spirits. They see a man from ancient times with a white face, which is a sign that they should not say anything untrue or do anything unfair. They also see a face in a window, which is a sign that they should leave. I too have seen that man from ancient times; and I too have seen the face in the window, and when I saw it, the spirits [from Jupiter] immediately left.

77 In addition to the spirits we have just been talking about, there are also spirits who argue in opposition. They were people who had been exiled from their communities during their lives in the world because they were evil. When they approach, you can see something like a flying flame that comes down close to their faces. They take a position down low, behind their subjects, and talk up at them from there.

They say things that go against what the teaching spirits said on behalf of the angels; for example, they say that there is no need for the people to live by what they are being taught, that they are free to do whatever they want. These spirits usually show up after the other spirits have left.

However, the people there know who these spirits are and what they are like, so they pay no attention to them. Still, though, they learn in this way what is evil and therefore what is good, since we learn what is good by means of what is evil. Indeed, the nature of anything good is recog-nized when we see its opposite. All our awareness of a particular thing comes from thoughtful attention to the features that distinguish it from things that contrast with it in various ways and to different degrees.

78 The punitive and teaching spirits do not come to the people who call themselves holy ones and mediating lords (the ones described in §70 above) as they do to the others on that planet. This is because these people do not allow themselves to be taught or to be corrected by any punishment. They are inflexible because self-love is what drives them. The spirits said that they recognize these people by their coldness, and that when they become aware of this coldness, they leave the people alone.

The spirits from Jupiter also include some whom they call chimney sweeps because the spirits in question dress like sweeps and have sooty faces as well. These too I am allowed to identify and describe.

79

One such spirit came up to me and earnestly begged me to intercede on his behalf so that he could get into heaven. He said that he was not aware of having done anything evil, only that he had rebuked people from his planet, adding that after he had rebuked them he had instructed them. He attached himself to my left side under the elbow. His voice cracked as he spoke. He was effective at evoking compassion, but all I could say in response was that I could not be of any help to him: that was up to the Lord alone. I could not intercede either, because I did not know whether it would be helpful or not; but if he was worthy, then there was hope for him. He was then sent to the company of some upright spirits from his own planet, but they said he could not be in their group because he was not upright. Since he kept demanding to be let into heaven so earnestly, though, he was sent to a community of upright spirits from our planet; but they too said that he could not be with them. He looked black in the light of heaven, though he himself said that he was not black but reddish brown.

[2] I was told that this is what the spirits are like at first who are later accepted among the ones who make up the province of the *seminal vesicles* in the universal human, or heaven. These vesicles are where the seed is collected and clothed with a substance which is able to prevent the fertility of the seed from being lost, but which can be shed at the entrance of the uterus so that what has been kept safe within will be effective for conception, or for impregnating the egg. So as a result, this seminal matter has a striving, an ardent desire, to shed itself and allow the seed to perform its proper function. You could see something of the sort in this spirit. He came to me again, in shabby clothing, and said again that he yearned to get into heaven, but added that he now began to perceive that he was the sort of spirit who could. I was given the inspiration to tell him that this might be a sign that he would be accepted before long. He was then told by some angels to take off his clothes. He was so eager that he did this faster than one would think possible, which was a representation of the eagerness of the spirits who are in the province that corresponds to the seminal vesicles.

[3] I was told that when people like this have been prepared for heaven they remove their old clothes and are dressed in gorgeous new garments, and become angels.

They are like caterpillars, which go through a humble state, but then change into nymphs and then butterflies and are given new clothes, so to speak, including wings of blue, yellow, silver, or gold. These creatures are then granted the freedom to fly through the air as their own heaven, to celebrate their marriages, and to lay their eggs—in this way providing for the continuance of their kind. At the same time they are allowed a sweet and elegant nourishment from the juices and scents of all kinds of flowers.

80 So far I have not described what the angels of this planet are like. The ones who come to the people of their planet and sit by their heads, as noted in §73 above, are not angels from their inner heaven but are angelic spirits or angels from their outer heaven. Since the nature of the angels [from their inner heaven] has also been disclosed to me, I wish to relate what I have learned about them as well.

[2] A particular spirit from Jupiter, one of the ones who strikes people with fear, came up to my left side under the elbow and spoke to me from there. His speech was raspy—the words were not very well articulated or distinct from each other, so it took some time before I could gather what he meant. Further, as he was speaking he was also creating an atmosphere of fear, warning me that when the angels came to me I should be sure to receive them graciously. I was permitted to reply, though, that this is not up to me—I am obligated to receive all people in accord with their nature.

[3] Soon afterward some angels from that planet arrived, and it was granted to me to perceive from the way they talked with me that they were entirely different from the angels of our planet. They communicated not through words but through mental images that spread out in all directions within me, and flowed from there into my face so that my face was reflecting every detail, beginning with my lips and spreading out from there in all directions. The images that took the place of words were separate from each other, but just barely so.

[4] Later on they communicated with me in another way, using images that were still less separated from each other, to the point that there seemed to be scarcely any spacing between them at all. To my perception it was like the meaning of verbal speech when someone ignores the words and pays attention solely to the meaning. This kind of communication was easier for me to understand than the earlier kind and was also fuller. Like the earlier kind, it flowed into my face, but the inflow, like the speech, was smoother; and unlike the earlier kind it began not with my lips but with my eyes.

[5] After that they communicated with me by a method that was even more smooth and full; but in that case my face could no longer keep up

and present a suitable motion. Rather, I felt an inflow into my brain, and felt that it was being moved in much the same way.

Lastly, they communicated in such a way that their message simply fell into my inner comprehension. It was like a stream of highly rarefied air. I felt the inflow itself, but did not get details with any clarity.

These kinds of speech behave like fluids of different kinds—the first like liquid water, the second like a thinner fluid, the third like the air [at sea level], and the fourth like the thinner air [at high altitude].

The spirit I mentioned earlier, the one by my left side, interrupted this from time to time, especially to remind me to be courteous to the angels. This was because there were spirits from our planet who kept saying things that displeased these angels. The spirit said that he had not understood what the angels were saying until he moved closer to my left ear. After that, his speech was no longer raspy, but sounded like that of other spirits.

Afterward I talked with these angels about things that are noteworthy on our planet, especially about our printing, about the Word, and about the various theological publications of the church based on the Word, saying that people here learn the Word and theological teachings because they are available in published form. The angels were utterly amazed that matters of this sort could be published in writing and in printed form. **81**

It was granted me to see what happens when spirits from that planet who have been prepared are taken up into heaven and become angels. Chariots and horses appear then, bright and fiery, which carry them up like Elijah [2 Kings 2:11]. The reason gleaming, fiery horses and chariots appear is that this is a representation of the fact that they have been taught and prepared to enter heaven, because chariots mean the teachings of the church and gleaming horses mean an enlightened understanding.[k] **82**

The heaven into which they are taken up can be seen to the right of their planet and therefore separate from the heaven of the angels from our planet. The angels in their heaven are seen to be dressed in brilliant **83**

---

k. Chariots mean the teachings of the church: 2762, 5321, 8215. Horses mean our understanding: 2760, 2761, 2762, 3217, 5321, 6125, 6400, 6534, 7024, 8146, 8148, 8381. The white horse in the Book of Revelation means an understanding of the Word: 2760. In a representative sense, Elijah means the Word: 2762, 5247; and since the Word is the origin of all the church's teachings and all its understanding, Elijah was called "the chariot of Israel and its cavalry" [2 Kings 2:12]: 2762. This is why he was carried up by a chariot and horses of fire: 2762, 8029.

blue, studded with golden stars. This is because they had loved that color in the world and believed it to be absolutely heavenly, especially because they are devoted to the particular kind of good and loving actions to which this color corresponds.[1]

 I saw a vision of a bald head, but only the top of it, which was bony; and I was told that the people on Jupiter who were going to die within a year saw a vision of this kind and then made their preparations. They have no fear of death there except as it involves leaving their spouses or children or parents, because they know that they will go on living after death; they are not leaving life, they are going to heaven. So they do not call dying "dying," but "being heavenized." As for the ones from that planet who have lived in true marriage love and have cared for their children as parents should, they do not die of illnesses but die peacefully, as if they were merely falling asleep. That is how they cross over from the world into heaven.

[2] Their usual lifespan is thirty years, going by our years. In the Lord's providence, they die after this short time to prevent the number of people there from rising beyond what that planet can support. Another reason is that once they have reached that age they no longer allow themselves to be led by spirits and angels the way the younger inhabitants do. As a result spirits and angels are rarely present with the older inhabitants. Then too, the people there mature more quickly than people on our planet do. They get married in the first flower of youth, and then their greatest joy is to love their spouse and care for their children. There are other things they call joys, but these are superficial by comparison.

The Planet *Mars* and Its Spirits and Inhabitants

85 THE spirits from Mars are among the best of all spirits from the planets in our solar system. Most of them are of a heavenly nature, not

---

1. Blue that contains a flamelike red corresponds to good actions that are motivated by heavenly love, while blue that contains a shining white corresponds to good actions that are motivated by spiritual love: 9868.

very different from the people who constituted the earliest church on our planet.ᵃ When I was shown images of their qualities, they were represented by a face in heaven and a body in the world of spirits, and in the case of the ones who were angels, by a face turned to the Lord and a body in heaven.

As spirits and angels see it, the planet Mars, like other planets in various locations, seems to have its own constant place—a little way out in front, to the left, at the level of the chest, and therefore outside the region where the spirits from our planet live.

The spirits from one planet are kept apart from the spirits of another planet because the spirits of each planet are associated with some particular district in the universal humanᵇ and are therefore in a different state. Difference of state makes them seem more or less widely separated from each other, either to the right or to the left.ᶜ

Spirits from Mars came to me and connected themselves to my left temple. There they breathed a communication toward me, but I could not understand it. The flow of their communication was very gentle—I had never felt one gentler, like the softest of breezes. It first reached my left temple and the top of my left ear, then moved on toward my left eye and gradually extended further toward the right, and flowed down, especially from my left eye, toward my lips; and once it reached my lips it followed a course into my mouth, and from a channel inside my mouth—the Eustachian tube in fact—it went into my brain. When the breath of their communication arrived there, then I became able to understand what they were saying and respond.

I noticed that when they were communicating with me my own lips would move and my tongue would also move a little. This is because there is a correspondence between inner and outer means of communication. By outer communication I mean that articulated sounds strike the membrane of the outer ear, and are then carried to the brain by means of the minute organs, membranes, and fibers that make up the inner ear.

---

a. The first and earliest church on our planet was a heavenly church, the finest of them all: 607, 895, 920, 1121, 1122, 1123, 1124, 2896, 4493, 8891, 9942, 10545 (which include descriptions). A church in which love for the Lord comes first is called "heavenly," while a church in which caring for the neighbor and faith come first is called "spiritual": 3691, 6435, 9468, 9680, 9683, 9780.
b. See note f on §5.
c. Distances in the other life are manifestations of realities that the Lord makes visible according to the deeper states of angels and spirits: 5605, 9104, 9440, 10146.

[2] This showed me that the method of communicating used by the inhabitants of Mars differs from that of the inhabitants of our planet in that theirs is not dependent on sound but is almost silent, making its way into the inner hearing and sight by a more direct route; and for this reason the communication is more complete, richer in thought imagery, and closer to the communication of spirits and angels. They use facial expressions to signal the emotional content of what they are saying, and they use their eyes to signal its thought content, because their emotions and facial expressions act in unison, as do their thoughts and what they are saying. To them it would be utterly reprehensible to think one thing and say another, or to have one thing in their heart and another on their face. They do not know what hypocrisy is, or what fraudulence and deception are.

[3] Conversations in the other life with some of the earliest people from our planet have made it possible for me to know that they had a similar method of communicating. To shed some light on this, let me relate what I have heard, as follows:

> By an inflow that I cannot describe, I have been shown how the people of the earliest church[d] communicated. Specifically, it was not articulated like the verbal speech of our own times but silent, using not external but internal breathing. This means that it was a thought-based form of communication. I was also allowed to perceive what their internal breathing was like: when they were communicating, it moved from the region of their navel to their heart and then through their lips, but without a sound. Further, it did not enter other people's ears from the outside and vibrate what is called the eardrum but came in by an inner route, in fact through what we now call the Eustachian tube.
>
> I was shown that this mode of communication enabled them to express their thoughts and opinions much more fully than can possibly be done using the articulated sounds of audible speech. Audible sounds, too, travel on breath (external breath, though), in the sense that there is no word or even part of a word that can be conveyed without the use of breath. The communication they had was much better, though, because it relied on internal breathing; and since the pathway was internal the communication was more perfect, more expressive, and better suited to the actual concepts of thought.

---

d. See note a on §85.

In addition, they used subtle movements of the lips and corresponding changes of facial expression. Since they were a heavenly kind of people, whatever they were thinking shone out from their face and eyes, and these would keep changing in response to their thoughts; their facial expressions and the gleam in their eye would reflect the liveliness of their emotions. They were completely incapable of making any facial expression that was at odds with their thinking. Since their mode of communication used internal breathing, which is the breathing of the human spirit, they were even able to communicate and interact with angels. [*Secrets of Heaven* 1118, 7361]

[4] The way the spirits from Mars breathe was also communicated to me.^e I became aware that their breathing started from the lower chest region toward the navel and flowed up from there through the chest, accompanied by an imperceptible movement of breath toward the mouth. This, together with other evidence from my experiences, made it possible for me to tell that they were of a heavenly nature and were therefore not unlike the people of the earliest church on this planet.

I have been informed that in the universal human, spirits from Mars relate to the connection between the understanding and the will, and therefore to *thoughts that arise from a feeling;* and the best of them relate to *the feeling behind the thoughts.* This is why their facial expressions act as one with their thinking and they are incapable of pretending otherwise to anyone.

Since that is what they are associated with in the universal human, the region that corresponds to them is the one that is between the cerebrum and the cerebellum. When the spiritual functioning of the cerebrum and of the cerebellum are united in people, their face acts in unison with their thoughts. Their face reveals the emotion behind what they are thinking, and that emotion, along with certain clues given off by the eyes, conveys the general tenor of their thinking. As a result, whenever these spirits were near me I actually felt as if the front of my head were being pulled toward the back, that is, the cerebrum were being pulled toward the cerebellum.^f

88

---

e. [Like us,] spirits and angels too have breathing: 3884, 3885, 3891, 3893.

f. In ancient times on our planet, people's faces were receptive to an inflow from their cerebellum; as a result, their faces reflected their inner emotions. Later, though, when people began to pretend and to use their facial expressions to counterfeit emotions they were not having, their faces became open to an inflow from their cerebrum. Information about changes in the way human faces operated over time: 4325–4328.

89   On one occasion, when some spirits from Mars were with me and were occupying the aura generated by my mind, some spirits from our planet came along with the intention of filling the same space. As they did so, though, the spirits from our planet became insane, because they were completely out of place. In the universal human, spirits from our planet play the role of the outer senses. They focus their attention on the world and themselves, while the spirits from Mars focus their attention away from themselves, on heaven and their neighbor; this was why there was opposition between the two groups. However, some angelic spirits from Mars arrived then and brought all communication between the groups to an end, so the spirits from our planet left.

90   The angelic spirits talked with me about the way the inhabitants of their planet live. They do not have any kind of government there but reside in separate communities, some of which are relatively large and some of which are small, and these communities are made up of people who share a similar disposition. The inhabitants recognize this similarity immediately from each other's faces and speech, and are rarely mistaken. They instantly become close friends.

The angelic spirits also said that the gatherings the inhabitants have are very enjoyable and that they talk about what is going on in their communities—especially about what is going on in heaven, since many of them have open communication with angels of heaven.

[2] If people in their communities begin to think dark thoughts and therefore intend to do evil, they are exiled and left to fend for themselves, so they live rather wretched lives outside any community, in rocky wastelands, since the others no longer show them support. Some of the communities will first try by various means to get these people to come to their senses, but when this proves fruitless, they leave them alone.

In this way they make sure that no craving for control or for excessive wealth creeps in, that is, that no one driven by a craving for control would take over one community and then many others, and no one driven by a craving for excessive wealth would take away others' belongings. They each live content with their own possessions and with the esteem they are given for being fair-minded and loving. This joy and peace of mind would be destroyed if people who think evil thoughts and have evil intent were not exiled and if the other inhabitants did not take strong, decisive action against self-love and love for the world at the very outset.

These are the loves that lead to kingdoms and empires, in which only a few have no desire to be in control or possess the wealth of others. This is because there are few who do what is right and fair out of a love for what is right and fair—and fewer still who do what is good because they are truly caring individuals. Instead, people do what is right and fair only because of fear—fear of the law, fear for their lives, or fear of losing their wealth, status, or reputation.

As for how the inhabitants of their planet view the Divine, they said **91** that they acknowledge and revere our Lord, saying that he is the only God and that he rules both heaven and the universe. They said as well that all that is good comes from him and that he leads them, and also that he often appears among them on their planet. I was then allowed to say that Christians on our planet too know that the Lord rules heaven and earth because of the words of the Lord himself in Matthew, "All power has been given to me in heaven and on earth" (Matthew 28:18), but that our people do not believe it the way people from Mars do.

[2] They also told me that the inhabitants believe there is nothing but what is foul and hellish in themselves and that all that is good comes from the Lord. The spirits added that they themselves are actually devils but that the Lord lifts them out of hell and constantly keeps them out.

[3] On one occasion, when someone mentioned the Lord by name, I saw those spirits humble themselves so deeply and profoundly as to defy description. In that state of humility they were thinking that left to themselves they are in hell and are therefore utterly unworthy to look toward the Lord, because he is holiness itself. Because of their beliefs they were so completely immersed in these thoughts that they were no longer in possession of themselves, remaining down on their knees, full of these reflections, until the Lord lifted them up and brought them out of hell, so to speak. When they come out of a humble state like this they are filled with goodness and love, and therefore feel joy in their hearts.

As long as they are bowing themselves down in humility like this they will not turn their face toward the Lord. They do not dare. They turn away. The spirits who were around me said that they had never seen such humility.

Some spirits from that planet were amazed that so many spirits from **92** hell were around me and were even talking to me; but it came to me to reply that they were allowed to do this so that I could know what they are like, why they are in hell, and that it is a result of the kind of life they had led. I was also allowed to mention that many of them were people I had known when they lived in the world and that some of them had been appointed to very high positions and yet at the time had cared about nothing but the world. I added that it was impossible for any evil spirit, even the most hellish, to do me any harm, because I was constantly protected by the Lord.

93 I was shown what an inhabitant of that planet looks like—what I saw, though, was not an actual inhabitant, but a likeness of one. His face was like the faces of inhabitants of our planet, but the lower part was black. This was not because of a beard, since he did not have one, but from a blackness where a beard would be; the blackness also extended to just below the ears on both sides. The upper part of the face looked tanned, like the faces of inhabitants of our planet that are not pale.

They said that on their planet they eat fruit from trees, and especially a kind of round fruit that grows out of their soil; they also eat vegetables. They wear clothes that they make from the fibers of the bark of particular trees that can be woven and also glued together with a kind of adhesive that they have.

They told me that they know how to make flammable liquids so that they have light in the evening and at night.

94 I saw a flame, as beautiful as could be. Its color varied—it had purple in it, and also red with bright areas, and the colors were sparkling because of the flame. I also saw a kind of hand to which the flame was clinging, first to the back of the hand, then to its cupped palm, after which the flame was licking the hand all around. This lasted for some time. Then the hand and the flame moved some distance away, and there was a brightness where it stopped. In that brightness the hand retreated, at which point the flame changed into a bird whose colors at first were like those of the flame and glistened in a similar way. Gradually, though, the colors changed, and as they did, so did the liveliness of the bird. It flew around, first circling my head and then flying forward into a kind of narrow chamber that looked like a shrine; but the farther forward it flew, the more its life drained away. Eventually it turned to stone, initially with a pearly color and then dark, but even though it had no life anymore, it still kept flying.

[2] Back when the bird was flying around my head and was still in the full flush of life, I saw a spirit coming up from below, through the region of the groin to the region of the chest. From that location he started trying to snatch the bird away. But since it was so beautiful, the spirits around me blocked him, because they were all transfixed, looking at the bird. However, the spirit who had come up from below argued forcefully that the Lord was with him and that he was therefore doing this on the

Lord's behalf. Even though most of them did not believe this, they no longer blocked him from taking away the bird; but since heaven flowed in at that moment, he could not keep hold of it, but soon released it from his hand and let it go free.

[3] When this was over, the spirits around me, who had been very closely watching the bird and the successive changes it went through, talked with each other about what had happened, and their discussion continued for a remarkable length of time. They were aware that a vision like this had to mean something heavenly. They knew that anything flamelike means heavenly love and the feelings that come from it, that the hand to which the flame was clinging means life and its power, and that changes in color mean variations in the wisdom and intelligence present in that life. They also knew that birds mean much the same thing, the main difference being that a flame means heavenly love and the feelings that come from it, while birds mean spiritual love and the feelings that come from that (heavenly love is love for the Lord; spiritual love is caring about one's neighbor).g They knew that changes in the bird's color and also in its liveliness until it turned to stone mean successive changes in understanding and their consequent impact on spiritual life. [4] They also knew that the spirits who come up from below through the region of the groin to the region of the chest are completely convinced that they are one with the Lord and therefore believe that everything they do, even if it is evil, is done in accord with the Lord's will.

Nonetheless, these spirits could not figure out which people were meant by the vision. Eventually they were told by a heavenly source that it was in reference to inhabitants of Mars. The flame that was clinging to the hand was a symbol for the many inhabitants who were still devoted to heavenly love. When the bird to begin with was in all its multicolored glory and in the full flush of life, it was a symbol for the inhabitants there who were devoted to spiritual love; but when the bird became stony and lifeless and when its color eventually darkened, it became a symbol for the inhabitants who had distanced themselves from doing good actions out of love and were instead engaged in evil, but in spite of that still believed that they were one with the Lord. The spirit who came up and tried to take away the bird meant much the same.

---

g. See note a on §85.

95   The bird of stone also represented particular inhabitants of that planet
who have a strange way of turning the vital energy of their thoughts and
feelings into something almost lifeless. The following is what I have heard
about this.

[2] There was once a spirit above my head who was speaking to me.
From the sound of his voice I could tell that he was in a sleeplike state.
Yet in that state he was saying many things and speaking as carefully as he
would have if he had been wide awake. I was given the perception that he
was an emissary through whom angels would speak, and that in that state
he would comprehend what the angels were saying and pass it on.[h] He
spoke nothing but the truth, though. If something flowed in from any
other source, he would indeed let it in but would not pass it on.

When I asked him about the state he was in he said that he experienced it as deeply peaceful and that he felt no anxiety whatever about the
future. Yet at the same time he was doing useful things that granted him
communication with heaven.

I was told that in the universal human, people like this are associated
with the brain's *longitudinal sinus,* which lies between its two hemispheres.
It remains in a quiet state there no matter how turbulent the brain becomes
on either side.

[3] While I was engaged in dialog with this spirit some other spirits
intruded toward the front part of the head where he was located. They
exerted pressure on him, so he withdrew to one side and let them have
the space.

These newly arrived spirits were talking with each other, but neither
the spirits around me nor I myself could understand what they were saying. I was told by some angels that they were spirits from the planet Mars
who knew how to talk with each other in such a way that nearby spirits
would not be able to perceive or understand anything they were saying.
I was surprised that there could be a way of communicating like this,
because all spirits share a common language that flows from their thinking and is made up of concepts that are heard as words in the spiritual
world. I was told, though, that these spirits have a method of expressing

---

h. Communication between one community of spirits or angels and others takes place by means
of spirits who are sent out to the other communities; these spirits who are sent out are called
"emissaries": 4403, 5856, 5983, 5985–5989.

concepts with their lips and faces in a way that is unintelligible to anyone else, and that they instantly and skillfully withdraw their thoughts, making particularly sure that no trace of feeling remains in evidence. If any trace of feeling were conveyed, the thinking would be exposed because thinking flows from feeling and is virtually contained within it.

I was told that this mode of communication was developed by inhabitants of Mars who define a heavenly way of life solely in terms of having knowledge and not in terms of living a life of love. (Not all the inhabitants there [share this view].) When these inhabitants become spirits they continue this mode of communication.

These individuals in particular are meant by the bird of stone, because to communicate in this way—by using facial expressions and curling their lips but keeping away from others what they are feeling and withdrawing their thoughts from them—is to take all the life out of their communication and make it like a statue. In fact, doing so gradually turns *them* into statues.

[4] But although they believe that others do not understand what they are saying to each other, angelic spirits have no difficulty perceiving absolutely everything they are saying. This is because no thought can be kept from this kind of spirit.

The spirits from Mars were in fact shown by firsthand experience that this is the case. I was thinking about the fact that evil spirits from our planet feel no shame when they are attacking others. This thought was actually flowing into me from angelic spirits who perceived that this was the topic being discussed by the spirits from Mars. The spirits from Mars were amazed at this and admitted that this was indeed what they had been talking about. In fact, just one angelic spirit was able to disclose much of what they were saying and thinking in spite of the fact that they were doing their best to hide their thoughts from him.

[5] Later these spirits flowed from above into my face. The inflow felt like streaks of light rain, which was a sign that they had no interest in anything true or good, since this disinterest is what streaks represent. Then they communicated with me clearly and said that [their covert mode of communication] was also how the inhabitants of their planet talked with each other.

They were then told that that type of communication is evil because they are blocking what is internal and moving away from it to what is external, and even that they are depriving it of its life. It is evil especially because it is dishonest to talk like this. Honest people do not want to say or even to think anything unless it is fit to be known by others—in fact by everyone, by all heaven. In contrast, people who pass judgment on others, thinking badly of them and highly of themselves, do not want others to know what they are saying. Eventually, habit drives such people to the point where they think and say bad things about the church, heaven, and even the Lord himself.

[6] They were also told that in the universal human, people who love knowledge but do not love living by it are associated with the inner membrane of the skull. People who have accustomed themselves to not communicating their feelings and to drawing their thoughts into themselves, keeping them from others, are also associated with that membrane, but one that has turned to bone, because whatever spiritual life they used to have becomes no life at all.

96 Since the bird of stone also represented people who were devoted solely to knowledge and not at all to living a life of love, and since this meant they had no spiritual life, as an appendix to this chapter I would like to point out that spiritual life is something possessed only by people who devote their lives to heavenly love and to the knowledge that goes with it. I will also show that every kind of love contains within itself a full cognitive capacity for the knowledge that goes with that love.

Take animals of the earth, for example, or those animals of the sky called birds. They have all the knowledge that supports what they love— their love of being nourished, living in safety, having offspring, nourishing their young, and for some, getting ready for winter. They have all the knowledge they need. That knowledge is actually inherent in what they love and flows into their love as into a container made specifically to hold it. Some animals even have a level of knowledge that we cannot help but find awe-inspiring. Animals are born with this knowledge. We call it "instinct," but it is actually a by-product of the earthly love that drives them.

[2] Love for the Lord and love for our neighbor are our proper loves, the loves that distinguish us from animals. They are heavenly loves. If we were devoted to these loves, then we would have not only all the knowledge we need but all the intelligence and wisdom as well, for they flow into these loves from heaven—that is, through heaven from the Divine.

However, since we are not born with these loves but with loves that oppose them, namely, love for ourselves and love for this world, we cannot help but be born into complete ignorance, knowing nothing. By divine means we are brought closer to intelligence and wisdom, but we are not really granted them unless our love for ourselves and love for this world are put aside and the way is thus opened for love for the Lord and love for our neighbor.

[3] We can tell that love for the Lord and love for our neighbor contain all intelligence and wisdom within them by the fact that when people who have been devoted to these loves in the world arrive in heaven after death, they know and appreciate things they had never known before. They actually think and talk like other angels, saying things no ear has heard or mind has known because they are ineffable. This is because these loves are by nature receptive to such things.

The Planet *Saturn* and Its Spirits and Inhabitants

THE spirits from that planet, like the planet itself, appear out in front at a considerable distance, down on a level with the knees. When one looks in that direction, a whole crowd of spirits comes into view, all of them from that planet. They are observed on the near side of that planet, toward the right. 97

I have been allowed to talk with them and from our conversation to learn what they are like in comparison to others. They are upright and modest; and since they think little of themselves, in the other life they actually look small as well.

The inhabitants of that planet are profoundly humble in their worship because in that context they think of themselves as nothing. They worship our Lord and acknowledge him as the only God. Further, the Lord sometimes appears to them in the form of an angel and therefore as human; and when this happens divinity shines forth from his face and moves their lower minds. 98

When the inhabitants come of age they talk with spirits, and the spirits teach them about the Lord, about how to worship, and about how to live.

When others try to lead the spirits from that planet astray and tear them away from their faith in the Lord, from their humble attitude toward him, and from their upright way of living, they say they want to die. Small knives then appear in their hands, with which they seem to be trying to stab themselves in the chest. When they are asked why they are doing this, they say they would rather die than be taken away from the Lord. Sometimes spirits from our planet make fun of them because of this and harass these upright spirits for behaving this way. The spirits reply, though, that they know perfectly well they are not actually killing themselves. This is just a projection that flows from what their lower mind desires: that they would rather die than be drawn away from their worship of the Lord.

99   They said that sometimes spirits from our planet come to them and ask what God they worship. They reply that the ones posing this question must be crazy. There could be nothing more insane than to ask what God someone worships when there is only one God for everyone in the universe; and they are even more insane for not saying that the Lord is that only God. He rules the whole heaven and therefore also rules the whole world; whoever rules heaven also rules the world because the world is ruled through heaven.

100   They said that there are some people on their planet who refer to the light they have at night (which is bright) as "the Lord," but these people are kept apart from the other inhabitants and are not tolerated by them. The light at night there comes from the great ring that surrounds their planet at some distance and from the satellites that are called Saturn's moons.

101   They told me that spirits of another type who travel in a group often come to them wanting to learn about their situation. These spirits use various means of finding out from them what they know. They said that these spirits are not crazy except in their being so eager to know things for no other reason than to know them. They were later told that these spirits were from the planet Mercury, the planet nearest to the Sun, and that knowledge itself is what they enjoy, and not any use they might get from it.

102   In the universal human, the inhabitants and spirits of Saturn have to do with *a sensory function midway between the spiritual and the earthly self,* but one that pulls back from the earthly self and draws closer to the spiritual self. Because of this these spirits seem to be borne or snatched up into heaven but are also soon sent back, since any sensory function that is spiritual occurs in heaven, while any sensory function that is earthly occurs underneath heaven.

[2] Since in the universal human the spirits of our planet have to do with the earthly and bodily senses, I learned from direct experience how the spiritual self and the earthly self fight and conflict with each other when

the earthly self is not devoted to faith and caring. [3] Some spirits from Saturn came into view at a distance, at which point a living communication was established between them and some spirits from our planet who were faithless and uncaring. As soon as the spirits from our planet became aware of the Saturnians they seemed to go crazy and began to harass them, deluging them with insults against their faith and against the Lord. While they were caught up in uttering these attacks and assaults, the spirits from our planet even broke into their midst and were driven so insane that they tried to do them harm. The spirits from Saturn felt no fear, though, because they were safe and at peace. But when our spirits were among these spirits from Saturn, our spirits began to feel pain and could not breathe, so they scattered in all directions and disappeared.

[4] We bystanders gathered from this what the earthly self that has been separated from the spiritual self is like when it enters a spiritual atmosphere—namely, that it becomes insane. This is because the earthly self that has been separated from the spiritual self derives all its wisdom from this world and none from heaven; and people who derive all their wisdom from this world believe only what is grasped by the bodily senses. This means that what they believe is based on fallacies arising from the senses, and if these are not put aside by an inflow from the spiritual world they lead to false conclusions. That is why spiritual matters mean nothing to people like this, even to the point that they can scarcely stand to hear the word "spiritual." As a result, when they are kept in a spiritual atmosphere they become insane. It is different while they are living in this world. They then either think materialistically about spiritual matters or turn their ears away—that is, they hear these things but pay no attention.

[5] This experience also showed that the earthly self cannot turn itself into the spiritual self—that is, it cannot rise up. However, when we are devoted to our faith and are therefore leading a spiritual life, our spiritual self flows into our earthly self and thinks there. There is such a thing as spiritual inflow, which is a flow from the spiritual world into the physical world, but there is no flow in the other direction.[a]

Spirits from that planet have also given me information about the **103** social structures of the people who live there, among other things. They

---

a. Inflow is spiritual and not physical or earthly, so there is an inflow from the spiritual world into the physical world but not from the physical into the spiritual: 3219, 5119, 5259, 5427, 5428, 5477, 6322. It seems as though there is an inflow from the outside into the inner self, but this is an illusion: 3721.

said that the inhabitants live divided into families, each family separate by itself, just a husband and wife with their children. When they marry they leave the home of their parents and are no longer concerned with it; therefore the spirits from that planet are seen in twos.

They do not make much fuss about food and clothing. They eat the fruits and vegetables that their land yields and their clothing is simple—they wrap themselves in a thick pelt or cloak that protects them from the cold.

Further, all the people on that planet know that they will go on living after death, so they attach little importance to their bodies—only as much as is necessary for living, which they call continuing to serve the Lord. For the same reason, too, they do not bury the bodies of their dead but discard them and cover them with tree branches from the forest.

104   Asked about the great ring that from the perspective of our planet appears to extend beyond that planet's circumference and to change where it appears over time, they said that to them it does not look like a ring but like a whiteness in various directions in their sky.

The Planet *Venus* and Its Spirits and Inhabitants

105   AS spirits and angels conceive of it, the planet Venus seems to be on the left, a little toward the back, not that far from our planet. I say "as spirits conceive of it" because neither the sun of our world nor any planet is visible to any spirit. Rather, spirits have only a concept of the existence of these things. Within the limits of their concepts concerning them, the sun of our world appears behind their backs as something dark, and the planets are not wandering as they do in our world but keep their places constantly (see §42 above).

106   There are two kinds of people on the planet Venus, of quite opposite dispositions. There are people who are gentle and humane, and there are people who are savage and almost feral. The gentle and humane ones appear [in the spiritual world] on the other side of that planet, while the savage, feral ones appear on the side that faces our planet. It is important to know, though, that these locations depend on their states of life, since the state of life determines all apparent space and distance in that world.

Some of the spirits who appear on the other side of that planet, the 107 gentle and humane ones, came to me and stood where I could see them, just above my head. I talked with them about various subjects. They said, among other things, that when they were in the physical world they had acknowledged our Lord as their only God and that now their acknowledgment was even greater. They insisted that they had seen him on their planet and even represented for me how they had seen him.

In the universal human, these spirits relate to *a type of memory of matter-based concepts that harmonizes with the memory of non-matter-based concepts* to which the spirits from Mercury relate. Because of this, spirits from Mercury are very much in harmony with spirits from Venus; so when they were together, I felt a distinct change in my brain and strong activity within it as a result of an inflow from them (see §43 above).

I have not talked with the spirits from the side of Venus that faces our 108 planet [in the spiritual world], the ones who are savage and almost feral. I have been told by angels, though, what they are like and where they get such a savage nature. They take great delight in pillage, and the greatest delight in eating plundered food. The pleasure they feel when they think about eating plundered food was communicated to me; I could tell that it was their supreme joy.

Historical accounts of various populations on our planet show that here as well there have been people this feral. Some of the inhabitants of the land of Canaan were this way (see 1 Samuel 30:16), as were some of the people of Judah and Israel at the time of David, who made annual forays to plunder other nations and rejoiced to eat the spoils.

I was told that most of these inhabitants of that planet were giants, and that the people of our planet would only come up to their navels.

I was also told that they are stupid, with no interest in heaven or eternal life. All they care about is what has to do with their land and their herds.

Because this is what they are like, when they come into the other life 109 they are completely overcome with evil and falsity.

Their hells can be seen near their planet. These hells have no contact with the hells of the evil from our planet because the two are of totally different natures and dispositions; therefore the types of evil and falsity in them are also totally different.

If they are capable of being saved, though, these spirits are taken to 110 places set aside for the process of devastation and there they are reduced to utter despair. This is because there is no other way that evil and falsity of this kind can be brought under control and put aside. When they are in a state of despair, they cry out that they are beasts, that they are loathsome, hateful, and therefore damned. Some of them even cry out against heaven when they are in this state, but this is overlooked in them because it is only an expression of their despair. The Lord makes sure, though, that their railing does not transgress certain limits.

When they have suffered the furthest extreme of the process, their self-centered, carnal appetites die, so to speak, and they are finally saved.

I was told concerning them that when they lived on their planet they believed in a Supreme Creator but without a mediator. As they are being saved, though, they are taught that the Lord is the only God, Savior, and Mediator.

I saw some of them, after they had suffered the worst, being carried up into heaven, and when they were accepted there I felt from them such a tender happiness that it brought tears to my eyes.

The *Moon* and Its Spirits and Inhabitants

111 ABOVE my head there once appeared some spirits from whom I heard voices like thunder. They made booming sounds exactly like the thunder that comes from the clouds after lightning. I assumed that this must be a great crowd of spirits, and they were particularly well practiced in making their voices sound like this. Some unsophisticated spirits who were with me, though, laughed out loud at these spirits, which was a real surprise to me. The reason for their laughter soon became clear—it was only a few spirits who were making this sound, not a great number, and they were as small as children. These spirits had used such sounds to terrify the spirits with me before, and yet they were completely incapable of doing any harm.

[2] So that I could learn what they were like, some of them came down from the height where they had been making these sounds. Much to my surprise, one was carrying another on his back, and in this fashion two of them came to me. Their faces were not unattractive, but were longer than the faces of other spirits. They were about as tall as seven-year-old children, but of sturdier build, so they were little people. I was told by some angels that they were from the Moon.

[3] The one carried by the other came to me, positioning himself at my left side under my elbow, and talked with me from there. He said that this is what they sound like when they use their voices, and that in this way they strike fear into spirits who want to do them harm, and even drive some of them away. This makes it possible for these spirits to go in safety wherever they wish. To convince me that this tremendous sound came from them, he went off to join some of his companions (without going completely out of sight) and thundered again.

They also showed me that belching the sound out of their abdomens gave it this thunderous quality. [4] I perceived that this practice arose out of the fact that the inhabitants of the Moon do not speak from their lungs like the inhabitants of other planets, but from the abdomen and therefore from some air that is stored there. This is because the Moon is not surrounded by the same kind of atmosphere as other planets are.

I was informed that in the universal human, spirits from the Moon have to do with the scutiform or xiphoid cartilage to which the ribs are attached in front and from which descends the fascia alba that supports the abdominal muscles.

Spirits and angels know that there are people living on the Moon just as there are on the moons of Jupiter and Saturn. Even the spirits who have not seen and talked with spirits from these moons have no doubt that there are people there because the moons are planets, too, and where there is a planet there are people. Humanity is, after all, the purpose for which planets exist, and the Supreme Creator has done nothing without a purpose. Anyone who thinks with even slightly enlightened reason can conclude that creation came about so that heaven could arise from humankind. **112**

Why the Lord Wanted to Be Born on Our Planet and Not on Some Other

THERE are many reasons why it pleased the Lord to be born and take on a human nature on our planet and not on some other, reasons about which I have been informed by a heavenly source. *The main reason* **113** *was for the sake of the Word, which was able to be written on our planet, and what was written was then able to be published throughout the whole planet; and once published, it was able to be preserved for all generations; and in this way it could become clear even to everyone in the other life that God had become a human.*

114   *The main reason was for the sake of the Word* because the Word is the divine truth itself that teaches humankind that God exists, that there is a heaven and a hell, and that there is a life after death. It also teaches how we must live and what we must believe if we are to come into heaven and live in happiness forever. All this would have been utterly unknown if there had been no revelation—which means, in the case of our planet, if there had been no Word—and yet with respect to our inner natures we have been created in such a way that we cannot die.[a]

115   *The Word was able to be written on our planet* because we have had the art of writing here since the earliest times, at first on wooden tablets, then on parchment, then on paper, and lastly in published form in print. This was provided by the Lord for the sake of the Word.

116   *The Word was then able to be published throughout the whole planet* because here commerce exists among all peoples, since we are able to travel not only by land but also by sea to all parts of the whole globe. So once the Word had been written it could be passed on from one people to another and taught everywhere.

117   *Once the Word was written down it was able to be preserved for all generations,* therefore for thousands and thousands of years; and as is well known, it has indeed been preserved.

118   *In this way it could become clear that God had become a human.* This is the first and foremost purpose of the Word, since no one can believe in a God and love a God who is incomprehensible because he has no specific manifestation. This is why people who worship God as an invisible and therefore incomprehensible entity lapse into thinking of nature as God and consequently believe in no God at all. For this reason it pleased the Lord to be born here and to make this fact clear by means of the

---

a. From earthly light alone, we know nothing about the Lord, heaven and hell, our life after death, or the divine truths that are essential for our spiritual and eternal life: 8944, 10318, 10319, 10320. Evidence for this is the fact that many people, including scholars, do not believe in these things even though they were born where the Word is present and have been taught from it about these matters: 10319. That is why it became necessary for there to be a revelation from heaven, since we are born for heaven: 1775.

Word—so that it might not only be known on this globe but could also *become clear as a result even to spirits and angels who have come from other planets, as well as to non-Christians who have come from our own.*[b]

It is important to know that the Word on our planet, which was given **119** by the Lord through heaven, is what unites heaven and the world. To this end there is a correspondence between everything in the literal sense of the Word and divine realities in heaven. It is also important to know that in its highest or deepest sense the Word is about the Lord, about his kingdom in the heavens and on earth, and about the love and faith we receive from him and return to him—that is, about the life we have from him and in him. Things like this are presented before the angels in heaven when the Word is read and preached on our planet.[c]

On all other planets, divine truth is revealed directly by spirits and **120** angels, as I have described above [§§65, 71, 73, 98] in discussing the inhabitants of planets in our solar system. This takes place within families, though, for on most planets humankind lives in separate families. This means that the divine truth revealed in this way through spirits and angels does not spread much beyond the family in which it was received, and if new revelations were not constantly occurring, the truth would become distorted or be lost. It is different on our planet, though, where the divine truth that is the Word remains in its integrity forever.

It is important to know that whatever planet people are from, the Lord **121** acknowledges and accepts everyone who acknowledges and worships a God in human form, because God in human form is the Lord. Since the Lord appears to the inhabitants of various planets in an angelic form, which is a human form, when spirits and angels from those planets hear from spirits and angels of our planet that God is an actual human being, they accept this as the Word, acknowledge it, and rejoice that this is the case.

In addition to the reasons just given, there is this: In the universal **122** human the inhabitants and spirits of our planet relate to the external,

---

b. In the other life, non-Christians are taught by angels; the non-Christians who have led good lives according to their religion are receptive to the truths of [Christian] faith and acknowledge the Lord: 2049, 2598, 2600, 2601, 2603, 2861, 2863, 3263.

c. The Word is understood differently by angels in the heavens than by us on earth: the meaning they take from it is internal and spiritual; the meaning we take from it is external and earthly: 1769–1772, 1887, 2143, 2333, 2395, 2540, 2541, 2545, 2551. The Word is what unites heaven and earth: 2310, 2895, 9212, 9216, 9357, 10375. Therefore the Word was written entirely by means of correspondences: 1404, 1408, 1409, 1540, 1619, 1659, 1709, 1783, 8615, 10687. In the deepest sense of the Word the only subject is the Lord and his kingdom: 1873, 2249, 2523, 7014, 9357.

physical senses, and these senses are the outermost limit, in which the deeper planes of life find completion, and on which they come to rest as their shared foundation. It is much the same with the presence of divine truth in the writing that we call the Word, which for this reason too was given on this planet rather than on any other.[d] Since the Lord is the Word and is the first and the last of it, he chose to be born and to become the Word on this planet so that everything would be done in accord with the divine design. This aligns with the following statements in John:

> In the beginning was the Word, and the Word was with God, and the Word was God. He was in the beginning with God. All things were made through him, and nothing that was made came about without him. *And the Word became flesh and lived among us; and we saw his glory, glory like that of the only-begotten child of the Father.* No one has ever seen God. The only-begotten Son, who is close to the Father's heart, has made him visible. (John 1:1, 2, 3, 4, 14, 18)

The Word is the Lord as divine truth, so it is divine truth from the Lord.[e] This, though, is a mystery that only a few will grasp.

---

d. In its literal meaning, the Word is earthly: 8783. This is because what is earthly is the outermost limit, in which spiritual and heavenly realities find completion and on which they stand as on their foundation; and because otherwise the Word's inner or spiritual meaning, lacking an outer or earthly meaning, would be like a house without a foundation: 9430, 9433, 9824, 10044, 10436.
e. The Word is the Lord as divine truth, so it is divine truth from the Lord: 2859, 4692, 5075, 9987. Everything was created and made by means of divine truth: 2803, 2894, 5272, 7678.

Extrasolar Planets

PEOPLE in heaven are able to speak and converse not only with angels 123 and spirits from the planets in our solar system but also with those who come from planets in the universe outside that system. They can communicate not only with the spirits and angels from these [extrasolar] planets, but also with the inhabitants themselves, though only with those whose inner reaches are opened so that they can hear people speaking from heaven.

We too can do the same while we are living in this world if the Lord allows us to talk with spirits and angels, since we ourselves are spirits as far as our inner selves are concerned. The bodies we carry around in this world simply enable us to function in this earthly or terrestrial realm, which is the outermost one. To communicate with spirits and angels as spirits ourselves, though, is allowed us only if our character is such that we can be in angelic company with respect to our faith and love; and we cannot be in that company unless our faith and love are focused on the Lord. This is because we are joined [to the Lord] through faith in him and love for him—that is, through truths we have been taught and good actions we have done that originate in him; and when we have been joined to him, we are safe from any assault of the evil spirits who come from hell. Other people's inner reaches cannot be opened that far because they are not in the Lord.

This is why there are not many people nowadays who are given the privilege of talking and interacting with angels. One clear sign of this is the fact that hardly any believe that spirits and angels even exist, let alone that they are with every one of us and that through them we have a connection with heaven and through heaven with the Lord. Still less do people believe that when our body dies we live on as spirits, and in just as human a form as before.

124　　　Since many in the present-day church do not believe in life after death and scarcely believe that heaven exists or that the Lord is the God of heaven and earth, the deeper levels of my spirit have been opened so that even while I am in my body I can at the same time be in the company of angels in heaven and not only talk with them but also see amazing things there and describe them. This is so that no one in the future will say, "Who has come from heaven to tell us that it exists and describe what is there?"

All the same, I am well aware that people who at heart have already denied the reality of heaven and hell and life after death will be adamantly opposed to these descriptions and will deny them, because it is easier to make a crow white than it is to make people believe something once they have rejected faith from their heart. This is because they constantly approach such matters from a negative perspective and not from an affirmative one.

What I have said and am about to say about angels and spirits is primarily for those few who believe. Nevertheless, in order that others too may be persuaded to accept at least a few of these ideas, I have been allowed to include the sort of details that appeal to and intrigue the curious. The next stories will be about extrasolar planets.

125　　　If you know nothing of heaven's secrets, you might not be able to believe that anyone could see such distant planets or report anything about them on the basis of direct experience. Be aware, though, that spaces, distances, and consequently movement from place to place in the spiritual world are, in their origins and first causes, inner changes of state, and that to angels and spirits, these spaces, distances, and movements appear in accordance with those inner changes.[a] Further, spirits and angels can by this means appear to be taken from one place to another and from one planet to another, even to planets that are at the edge of the universe. The spirit of a person in this world can also do this, even while the person's body remains in the same place.

That is what has happened with me, since by the Lord's divine mercy it has been granted to me to talk with spirits as a spirit and at the same

---

a. In the other life, [what spirits and angels experience as] motion, travel, and changes of location are actually changes in the inner state of their lives, and yet the relocation appears to the spirits and angels to be perfectly real: 1273–1277, 1377, 3356, 5605, 10734.

time with people on earth as a person on earth. The fact that our spirit can travel in this way is not something sense-oriented people can grasp, because they are immersed in space and time and measure their journeys by these criteria.

Anyone can conclude that there are many solar systems from the fact that we can see so many stars in the universe. It is common knowledge in the learned world that each star is a sun in its own region, remaining fixed the way the sun of our planet does in its own position, and only their great distance from us makes stars appear small. So we may conclude that like our sun, each star has planets around it that are worlds. We cannot see them with our eyes because they are at a vast distance from us and because the light they have from their star is not strong enough to be reflected all the way to us.

126

What other use could there be for such a huge expanse of space and so many stars? After all, the purpose of the creation of the universe is humankind and, through humankind, a heaven of angels. If the human race and the resulting angelic heaven came from just one planet, how would that satisfy an infinite Creator, for whom a thousand planets or even millions would not be enough?

[2] I once calculated that if there were a million planets in the universe, with three hundred million (300,000,000) people on each planet, and two hundred generations over six thousand years, and if each individual or spirit were given a space of three cubic ells, then the total of all these people or spirits gathered into one place would not fill the space of a thousandth part of this planet—perhaps the space, then, of one of the moons of Jupiter or of Saturn. This would be an almost invisibly small space in the universe—we can scarcely see those moons with the naked eye. What would this be for the creator of the universe, for whom it would not be enough if the whole universe were full? The Creator is, after all, infinite.

[3] I discussed this with angels and they said they have a similar idea of the meager extent of the human race in comparison to the infinity of the Creator, although they think of it in terms of states rather than of space; to their minds, no matter how many millions of planets one could ever imagine, they would still be absolutely nothing compared to the Lord.

But the source of the material that follows about extrasolar planets is [not theory or imagination but] my own personal experience. Among other things the accounts will show how my spirit traveled to those planets while my body stayed where it was.

A First Extrasolar Planet
and Its Spirits and Inhabitants,
Based on Things I Heard and Saw for Myself

127 ANGELS who had been sent by the Lord took me to a particular extrasolar planet, where I was allowed to observe the planet itself, but not to speak with its inhabitants—although I was allowed to speak with spirits who came from there. After their lives in the physical world come to an end, all the people who inhabit a given planet become spirits and remain in the general neighborhood of their planet. They are still able, therefore, to be a source of information about their planet and the state of the people who live there, because when we leave our bodies we take with us our whole former life, including our whole memory.[a]

[2] Being taken to other planets in the universe does not mean being taken there in the body, but rather in the spirit, which is led through changes of the state of its inner life that seem like movement through space.[b] What enables people to approach each other is harmony or similarity in the states of their lives, because harmony and similarity bring people together, and discord and dissimilarity drive them apart. As a result, a person's spirit can be transported and brought to distant places while the person remains in the same place.

[3] Only the Lord, though, has the power to lead our spirit outside its usual sphere through changes of our inner state. Only he can bring it about that these changes follow a sequence that leads to a state of harmony or similarity with the people to whom we are being led. This requires foresight and constant guidance from beginning to end, there and back,

---

a. After death we retain a memory of all our dealings in the world: 2475–2486.
b. See note a on §125.

and this is especially true in the case of people who are still bodily present in the material world, and are therefore in [time and] space.

[4] This actually happened to me, but if people are completely absorbed in their physical senses and do their thinking on that basis, there is no way to get them to believe that. This is because the physical senses cannot grasp the idea of travel without moving through space. If people do their thinking on the basis of the senses of their spirit, though, at least somewhat above and away from the senses of their body, and therefore think inwardly, they can be led to believe and grasp this, because there is no space or time in the concepts of deeper thought. Instead, there are the properties that underlie space and time.

The following material about extrasolar planets is for people like this, then, and not for others unless they are by nature willing to learn.

While I was awake, angels from the Lord led my spirit to a particular planet in the universe; we were accompanied by some spirits from our planet. We advanced to the right for two hours.   **128**

At the outer limit of our solar system the first thing I saw was a dense yet shining cloud, and beyond that there was fiery smoke rising out of a huge abyss. This was a vast chasm separating this side of our solar system from some extrasolar planets. As we traveled a considerable distance we kept seeing the fiery smoke.

I was taken across the middle of it, and in the abyss or chasm below me I saw many people, meaning spirits (all spirits have a human form and are actually people). I heard them talking with each other but it was not granted me to know where they were from or what they were like. One of them said to me, though, that they were guards to prevent anyone from crossing from our solar system to another one without permission. I was also given proof that this was the truth. When some of the spirits in our company who lacked permission to cross over came to that great abyss they began screaming that they were dying. They looked like people in the grip of death. So they stayed on their side of the chasm and could not be taken across. It was actually the smoke billowing from the chasm that overcame them and caused this torment.

After being taken across that vast abyss I finally reached a place where I could stop for a while. Some spirits then appeared above me, and I was able to talk with them. From their manner of speaking and their unique way of perceiving things and expressing their views I could clearly tell that they were from an extrasolar planet, since they were completely different from the spirits of our solar system. They could also tell from my speech that I was from far away.   **129**

130 After we had some conversation on various subjects, I asked them what God they worshiped. They said that actually they worship a particular angel, an angel who looks to them like a divine person, radiant with light. This angel teaches them and helps them see how they should be living their lives. They know, they added, that God Almighty is in the sun of the angelic heaven and that although he does not appear to them, he does appear to their angel; but he is too powerful for them to dare to worship him.

The angel they worshiped was actually a whole angelic community, to which the Lord had assigned the task of overseeing them and teaching them the path of justice and uprightness. The light these spirits have as a result is yellow and fiery, like the light of a burning torch, because the object of their adoration is not the Lord himself. Therefore the light they have is not the light of the sun in the angelic heaven but just light from that particular angelic community. When the Lord so provides, an angelic community can shed light on spirits who are in a lower region.

I was able to see that angelic community. It was high above them. I also saw in that community the flame that gave these spirits their light.

131 As for their other qualities, they were modest, rather simple people, but their thinking was quite good. I was able to determine what their faculty of understanding was like from the light that they had, since the understanding we have depends on how receptive we are to the light that exists in the heavens. This is because the divine truth that radiates from the Lord as the sun is what gives light there and makes it possible for angels not only to see but also to understand.[c]

132 I was informed that in the universal human the inhabitants and spirits of that planet have to do with something in the *spleen*, and this was confirmed for me by an inflow into my spleen when they were talking with me.

133 When I asked them about the sun of their solar system, which gives light to their planet, they said that the sun there looks fiery. When I showed them the size of the sun of our planet they stated that their sun was smaller. (Of course, to our eyes their sun is a star.) From angels as well I heard that their star is one of the smaller ones.

---

c. There is a great abundance of light in the heavens: 1117, 1521, 1522, 1533, 1619–1632, 4527, 5400, 8644. All the light in the heavens comes from the Lord as the sun: 1053, 1521, 3195, 3341, 3636, 4415, 9548, 9684, 10809. The divine truth that radiates from the Lord becomes manifest in the heavens as light: 3195, 3222–3224, 5400, 8644, 9399, 9548, 9684. That light enlightens both the vision and the understanding of angels and spirits: 2776, 3138. Heaven's light is also what enlightens the understanding of people [in the physical world]: 1524, 3138, 3167, 4408, 6608, 8707, 9128, 9399, 10569.

They added that from their planet they too see a star-studded sky and that there is a star larger than the rest that they see toward the west. I was told by a heavenly source that it is our sun.

After a little while my sight was opened so that I could look at their **134** actual planet to some extent, and I saw multiple meadows, deciduous forests, and woolly sheep.

Then I saw some of the people who lived there, of the more lowly sort, who were dressed quite similarly to country people in Europe. I saw a husband and wife. She was good-looking and graceful, and so was her husband; but what surprised me was that he strode with an air of nobility as if there were pride in his step, but his wife walked humbly. I was told by angels that this was the custom on that planet and that men like that are well loved there because they are nonetheless good people. I was further told that they are not allowed to have more than one wife, because this is against the law.

The woman I saw wore over her chest a garment wide enough to allow her to conceal the rest of her body by inserting her arms through it and wrapping it around herself. She could then go on her way. The lower part of it could be folded up and fastened so that the garment looked like the stomachers that women on our planet wear. The same garment also served as clothing for the man, though. I saw him take it from the woman and put it on his back, loosening the lower part so that it hung down to his feet like a toga, and walking around in it.

What I saw on that planet I did not see with my physical eyes but with the eyes of my spirit; and our spirit can see things that are on a physical planet when allowed to do so by the Lord.

Since I know that some people are not going to believe that anyone **135** could ever see anything on such a remote planet with the eyes of the spirit, let me explain how this works.

Distances in the other life are not like distances on earth. Distances in the other life depend entirely on the inner states of the people in question. The people who live together in a given community there and inhabit the same region are people whose states are similar. Presence there depends entirely on similarity of state, and distance is a function of dissimilarity. So when the Lord led me into a state like the state of that planet's spirits and inhabitants, then I was near that planet, and once I was there I was able to talk with them. This shows that in the spiritual world planets are not distant from each other in the same way they are in the material world but only seem so because of the states of life of their inhabitants and spirits; and by "states of life" I mean the state of the love and the faith contained in their hearts.

Let me also explain how it is that a spirit—or what is the same thing, a person functioning in the spirit—can see things on another planet. [2] With their own vision, neither spirits nor angels can see anything at all in the physical world. In fact, for them the light of our world, the light of its sun, is like thick darkness. By the same token, we cannot see anything at all in the other life with our physical vision. For us the light of heaven is like thick darkness.

When it pleases the Lord, though, a spirit or an angel can see things in the physical world through our eyes. However, this happens only if we are people allowed by the Lord to talk with spirits and angels and to associate with them. Through my eyes they have been permitted to see things in the world just as clearly as I do, and to hear the people who were talking with me as well. It has happened several times that they have seen through me some of the friends they had had in the world. Looking through my eyes they were stunned to be able to see their friends so close at hand. They have even seen their spouses and children and have wanted me to say that they were present and able to see them; they wanted me to tell their loved ones about their state in the other life. I have been strictly forbidden, however, to say this or to reveal that they were being seen. Among other considerations, the loved ones would have said I was insane or would have thought I was hallucinating. I am well aware that even though people say with their mouths that spirits are real, and that the dead have been raised and are with the spirits and can see and hear through us, in their hearts they do not believe it.

[3] When my inner sight was first opened, the people in the other life who saw the world and what was happening in it through my eyes were so stunned that they called it the miracle of miracles. They were moved by a new joy that this kind of communication of earth with heaven and of heaven with earth was being provided. This joy lasted for several months, but now that the phenomenon has become familiar they no longer marvel at it.

I have been told that the spirits and angels who are with other people see nothing whatever of what is happening in the world but are aware only of the thoughts and feelings of the people they are with.

[4] These experiences made it clear that we have been created in such a way that while we are living among others in this world we could also be living among angels in heaven and they could be living among us. In this way heaven and the world would coexist and work together in us. We would know what was happening in heaven and angels would know what was happening in the world; and when we died, we would cross over from the Lord's kingdom on earth into the Lord's kingdom in the heavens.

This would not be like passing from one kingdom into another but like passing into the same one we already inhabited during our physical lives.

Instead we have become so focused on bodily things that we have shut heaven off from ourselves.

Later I told some spirits from that planet about various things that exist on our planet, especially about our having sciences that others do not—astronomy, geometry, engineering, physics, chemistry, medicine, optics, philosophy. I also told them about technologies we have that are unknown elsewhere: for example, shipbuilding, metal casting, writing on paper, printing and publishing, and using books not only to communicate with others currently alive on our planet but also to preserve the written word thousands of years into the future. I told them that this has been done with the Word given us by the Lord, and that as a result revelation remains constant on our planet.

Eventually I was shown the hell for people from that planet. The people there were absolutely terrifying. I dare not describe their monstrous faces. I also saw women there who practice malignant sorcery. They appeared in green clothing and filled me with a sudden horror.

A Second Extrasolar Planet
and Its Spirits and Inhabitants

LATER on, I was taken by the Lord to a planet out in space that was farther from our planet than the first one, the one just discussed. I could tell it was farther away because it took my spirit two whole days to be led there. This planet was to the left, while the former one was to the right.

As I said before [§§125, 127, 135], remoteness in the spiritual world arises not from distance between locations but from a difference in state. Therefore I could tell from the slowness of my trip there—two days—that the inner state of its spirits (the state of their feelings and consequent thoughts) was significantly different from the inner state of the spirits of our planet.

Since I was taken there in spirit by changes in my inner state, I had a chance to observe the actual changes as they followed one another until I arrived. This happened while I was awake.

139   When I got there I did not see the planet itself, but I did see some spirits from it, since as already noted [§127] the spirits of any planet can be seen in its vicinity. This is because they have a nature similar to that of the planet's inhabitants, they once lived there themselves, and the current inhabitants need their help.

I saw these spirits fairly high above my head, and from there they saw me clearly as I arrived. It is important to know that in the other life people who are located on high can clearly see people who are below them, and the higher they are, the wider their view; and they can not only see people but communicate with them as well.

They observed that I was not from their planet but from somewhere quite remote; so they addressed me from where they were, asking me various questions to which I was allowed to respond. I told them among other things what planet I was from and what it was like; and later I told them about other planets in our solar system. I included a mention of the spirits from Mercury who travel around to many other planets gaining knowledge for themselves about various things. When they heard this, they said that they too had been visited by them.

140   I was told by some angels from our world that in the universal human the inhabitants and spirits of this planet have to do with *keenness of vision,* which is why they are seen on high, and that they actually are very sharp-sighted.

Because this is what they relate to and because they have such a clear sight of what is below them, in the course of our conversation I compared them to eagles, which fly high and see clearly far and wide. This upset them, though, because they thought I believed them to be predatory like eagles and therefore evil; but I replied that I was comparing them to eagles not as predators but rather as having clear sight.

141   Asked about what God they worshiped, they answered that they worshiped a God both visible and invisible—a visible God in human form and an invisible God in no form at all. Both from what they said and from thought images they shared with me, I learned that their visible God was our Lord himself and that they too called him "the Lord."

It occurred to me to respond that on our planet too a God both visible and invisible is worshiped; the invisible God is called "the Father," and the visible God is called "the Lord." The two are one, though, as the Lord himself taught when he said that people have never seen what the Father looks like, but that the Father and he are one, that those who see him see the Father, and that the Father is in him and he in the Father. So both divine attributes exist in one person.

To see that these are the words of the Lord himself, look at John 5:37; 10:30; 14:7, 9, 10, 11.

Later I saw some other spirits from that same planet who appeared **142** in a place below the spirits just mentioned; I talked with them as well. They were idolaters; they worshiped a stone idol that looked more or less human, but was not pleasing to look at. It is important to know that the religious focus of all who arrive in the other life is at first the same as it was in the world; they are weaned from it only gradually. This is because our whole religious orientation is deeply rooted in our inner life, and it takes time to uproot and remove it from that life.

When I saw their idolatry, it occurred to me to tell them that they should worship what is living, not what is dead. They replied that they know God is alive and is not made of stone, but by focusing their attention on the human-shaped stone they think about the living God; there is no other way they can fix and focus the ideas of their thought on a God who is invisible.

It then came to me to say that the ideas of their thoughts could in fact be fixed and focused on a God who is invisible if they were focused on the Lord, who is a God visible to our thoughts in a human form. In this way, by being joined to the Lord we can be joined to the invisible God in thought and feeling and therefore in faith and love. It cannot happen in any other way.

I asked the spirits overhead whether on their planet they lived under **143** the dominion of rulers and monarchs. They replied that they did not even know what that meant. They live on their own, distinguished into peoples, extended families, and individual households. Asked whether it was safe for them to live that way, they said that it was, because there was nothing one extended family had that another family envied or wanted to take away. In fact, it bothered them that I asked, as though I were imply-ing they were hostile to each other or needed protection from thieves. What more did they need, they insisted, than to have food and clothing and to live quietly and contentedly on their own?

In response to further questions about their planet, they said that they **144** had meadows, flower gardens, woods full of fruit trees, and lakes with fish in them; also blue-colored birds with golden wings, and animals large and small. They mentioned that one of their smaller animals is humpbacked, like the camels on our planet. The only meat they eat, however, is fish. They also eat fruit from their trees and vegetables from their soil.

They said they did not live in human-built houses but in groves where they made roofs for themselves among the branches as protection from the rain and from the heat of the sun.

145   When I asked them about their sun, which to our eyes on Earth is a star, they said that it looked fiery and appeared no larger than a human head. I was told by angels that the star that is their sun is one of the smaller stars and is not far from the celestial equator.

146   I saw some spirits from that planet who looked the same way they had during their lives there. Their faces are not all that different from the faces of people on our planet except that their eyes and noses are small. This made their faces look distorted to me, but they explained that they consider small eyes and a small nose to be most beautiful.

    I saw a woman wearing a robe that had on it roses of various colors. I asked what they make their clothing from, and they replied that they take plant material and make it into threads, then place the threads together in double or triple layers and moisten them with an adhesive fluid so that they hold together. They then color the fabric with vegetable dyes.

    I was also shown how they make their thread. They sit half-reclined in a chair and twist the thread with their toes, then pull the twisted thread toward themselves and work it with their hands.

147   They said that on that planet a husband has only one wife, no more, and that a couple will have ten or even fifteen children. They added that there are prostitutes there as well, but that when they become spirits after their physical lives they take up sorcery and are cast into hell.

A Third Extrasolar Planet
and Its Spirits and Inhabitants

148   SOME spirits appeared at a distance but were reluctant to come closer. This was because they could not be in the same place as the spirits from our planet who were with me at the time. I gathered from this that they were from another planet; and later I was told that they were from an extrasolar planet, although I was not told where that planet was.

    These spirits absolutely refuse to think about their bodies or even about anything physical or material, unlike spirits from our planet. That was why they did not want to come any closer. All the same, when some of the spirits from our planet left they did come closer and talk with me; but even then I could feel an anxiety occasioned by the collision of auras.

There are spiritual auras around every individual spirit and also around all communities of spirits,[a] and since these auras radiate from the life of their feelings and associated thoughts, wherever there are contrary feelings there is a collision and therefore anxiety.

The spirits from our planet told me that they too did not dare approach these others, because when they tried they were not only seized with anxiety but even appeared to be bound hand and foot by serpents, and were unable to be rid of the serpents unless they retreated. This appearance can be attributed to a correspondence, since in the universal human, spirits from our planet play the role of the outer senses—meaning bodily sensations—and in the other life the outer senses are represented by serpents.[b]

Since that is the nature of the spirits from that planet, in the eyes of other spirits they do not appear in a clearly defined human form the way others do; instead they look more like clouds. Many of them look like black clouds with a shining, vaguely human shape showing through here and there. They said, though, that inwardly they shine brightly and that when they become angels the [outward] darkness turns into a beautiful, heavenly blue—a phenomenon they also showed me. **149**

I asked them whether they had had the same low opinion of the body when they were people living in the physical realm. They said that the people of their planet attach no importance to their bodies, only to the spirit within the body, because they know that the body will die but the spirit will go on living forever. Many of the inhabitants, they said, believe that the spirit within the body has existed forever and is poured into the body at conception; but they added that they themselves now know this is not the case and regret having had such a mistaken opinion.

When I asked whether they would like to see some of the things on our planet and said that this could be done through my eyes (see §135 above), they answered at first that this was impossible and then that they **150**

---

a. See note g on §64.

b. In the spiritual world our outer senses are represented by serpents because they are on the lowest level, and in relation to the deeper aspects of our being they lie on the ground and seem to slither; and this is why people who do their reasoning on the basis of their senses are called serpents: 195, 196, 197, 6398, 6949.

did not want to, because all they would see would be earthly and material things, which they did their best to exclude from their thinking.

Nevertheless, they were shown representations of some splendid mansions like the ones monarchs and rulers have on our earth, since things like this can be represented to spirits, and these representations are so vivid that it is just as though the objects were right there. However, the spirits of that planet were not in the least impressed. They said these were just imitations made of marble. Then they told me that they had even more splendid structures and that these were their sacred gathering places, made not from stone but from wood.

When I said that these structures were nonetheless earthly they said no, they were heavenly because when they looked at them their mental image was of something heavenly, not earthly. They believed that they would also see things like this in heaven after their death.

151   Then their sacred gathering places were shown to some spirits from our planet; they said that they had never seen anything more magnificent. I saw them too, and can therefore describe them. These structures are made from trees that have not been cut down but are still growing in their native soil. The spirits said that on that planet they have trees that grow wonderfully tall and large. They plant these in patterns right from the beginning to become covered walkways, and while their branches are still pliable, well in advance they trim and prune them so that as they grow they will intertwine and join together to form the subfloor and the finish flooring of the developing structure and will also grow up on the sides to form walls, eventually bending together into arches overhead to form the roof. In this way, with amazing skill, they form a structure that is raised high above the ground, and provide it with a staircase formed of branches extending out and solidly connected. They also decorate the space in various ways outside and in by bending branches into particular forms. They make whole groves like this.

I was not allowed to see what their sacred gathering places looked like on the inside, though. I was told only that their sun's light is let in through spaces between the branches and refracted in all directions by crystals that vary the light on the walls in rainbowlike colors—especially shades of blue and orange, which they love the most.

This was their architecture, which they preferred to the most magnificent mansions on our planet.

152   They went on to say that the inhabitants do not make their *dwellings* in lofty places, though, but instead in lowly huts on the ground, because lofty places are for the Lord who is in heaven and lowly places are appropriate for people in the physical world. They showed me their huts. They were rectangular. Inside, there was a long bed along the wall where they lay head to toe. Opposite the door was a circular area with a table at the front and a fireplace at the back that lit up the whole room. No flames burned on the hearth, though; instead there was some luminous wood that gave as much light as the fire on any hearth. They said that in the evening these logs look as though they have burning embers within them.

They said that they do not live in communities but household by household, and that they are together in one community only when they gather for worship. Then the ones who teach walk around in the area under the raised structure, while the others are in the covered walkways to the sides. They said that they find deep joy in these meetings, both from seeing their gathering place and from worshiping in it. **153**

As to how they view the Divine, they said that they acknowledge God in human form—that is, our Lord. Anyone who acknowledges the God of the universe in human form is welcomed by our Lord and led by him. Others cannot be led by him because their thought about God has no focus. **154**

The inhabitants of their planet, they went on to say, are taught about matters of heaven by a form of direct contact with angels and spirits. They are led by the Lord into such contact more easily than others are because they banish material preoccupations from their thinking and feeling.

I asked what happens to those among them who are evil. They said that on their planet people are not allowed to behave immorally. If any of them think evil thoughts and do evil things, they are rebuked by a particular spirit who threatens them with death if they persist in what they are doing; and if they do persist, they lose consciousness and die. This is how the people of that planet are protected from the spread of evil.

One such spirit was sent to me and talked to me as though I were an inhabitant of that planet. He also caused a kind of pain in my abdominal region, saying that this was what he did to people who were contemplating or doing evil, and that he would threaten them with death if they persisted.

The spirits also said that people who profaned holy things were even more severely punished and that before the punitive spirit came to them they would have a vision of the gaping jaws of a lion, pale as a corpse, who seemed to be trying to swallow their head and wrest it from their body. This overwhelmed them with terror. They called this punitive spirit a devil.

155　　Since they wanted to know how revelation worked on our planet, I told them that it was given through writing and through preaching from the Word and not by direct contact with spirits and angels. I also told them that what is written can be published in print and read and understood by whole populations, to the amendment of their lives. It quite astonished them that we have this technology, which is absolutely unknown anywhere else; but they understood that on a planet where there is such a love for things physical and earthly, there is no other way divine teachings can flow in from heaven and be accepted, and that it would actually be dangerous for such people to talk with angels.

156　　The spirits from that planet can be seen high up, at head level, toward the right. All spirits can be identified by their position relative to the human body. This is because heaven in its entirety corresponds to a human being in every detail.[c] These spirits stay on that level and at that distance because they correspond not to outer features of a person but to inner ones. Their activity affects the left knee, above and a bit below, with a very noticeable trembling. This is an indication that they correspond to *the joining together of what is earthly and what is heavenly*.

A Fourth Extrasolar Planet
and Its Spirits and Inhabitants

157　　I was taken to yet another planet out in space beyond our solar system, a journey accomplished by changes in the state of my mind and therefore with regard to my spirit. As I have already said several times [§§125, 127, 135], the only way spirits can be taken from place to place is by changes in their inner state. To the spirits themselves, these changes look exactly like going from place to place, like traveling. I experienced changes like this steadily for about ten hours until I had left behind my own

---

c. See note f on §5.

state of life and had come into theirs, meaning that I arrived there in spirit.

Along the way I was taken eastward, toward the left, and seemed to be gradually lifted up above the horizontal plane. I was also able to observe quite clearly a progress and motion away from my former location, even to the point that I could no longer see the people I had left behind. While this was going on, some spirits were accompanying me, and I talked with them about various matters.

One of the spirits who was with us had been a church leader during his earthly life, and also a deeply moving preacher and writer. My companion spirits gathered from my own image of him that he was at heart more of a Christian than others, since in the world we form our image of others and judge them on the basis of what they preach and write and not on the basis of how they live their life, if this is not known to us. But even if something in their life were to seem inconsistent with their message, we would overlook it anyway. This is because our image of others, what we already think and feel about them, always colors any new information we receive about them.

Once there, I realized that in spirit I was somewhere among the stars far outside our solar system. This I could tell from the changes of state and from my seeming to have traveled continuously for almost ten hours. Eventually I heard some spirits talking near a planet that I later saw for myself. When I approached them, after we had some conversation together they said that sometimes visitors come from elsewhere who talk to them about God and give them confusing mental images. They showed me the direction from which these visitors arrived, and I gathered that they were spirits from our planet. Asked about the nature of the confusion, they replied that it was because these visitors said we should believe in a Divinity divided into three persons, whom the visitors nevertheless referred to as one God. When the spirits of that planet examined the mental image their visitors had in their minds, it was revealed to be a trinity that was not interconnected but divided. The picture some of the visitors had was of three separate beings in conversation, and one would talk to another. Other visitors were picturing two beings sitting side by side with a third listening to their conversation and then departing from them; but although they called each person God and had a different mental image of each one, they still spoke of them as "one God."

The spirits of that planet complained bitterly that this confused them, this thinking three and saying one, when what we think should agree with what we say and what we say should agree with what we think.

158

[2] The spirit with me who had been a church leader and preacher in the world was then examined to see what image he had regarding one God and three persons. He represented before us three gods who were nevertheless one by virtue of their interconnectedness; but his thinking portrayed this united trinity as invisible because it was divine. When he presented it this way, we perceived that he was then thinking only of the Father and not of the Lord, and that his image of the invisible God was nothing but an image of nature in its first principles. This meant that as far as he was concerned, what lay deeply hidden within nature was his concept of the Divine and that therefore he could easily be persuaded to acknowledge nature as God.

It is important to know that in the other life whatever mental picture we have of anything is vividly put on display. This is what makes it possible for each of us to be examined with respect to the nature of our thought and perception about matters of faith. The image we have when we think about God is absolutely fundamental. This is because if it reflects reality, it allows us to be joined to the Divine and therefore also to heaven.

[3] I asked the spirits from that planet what their image of God was. They answered that they thought of God not as invisible but as visible in human form. They knew this not only on the basis of an inner perception but because God had actually appeared to them in human form. They added that if they were to conceive of God as invisible the way these visitors did, as having no form or nature, there was no way they could think about God at all, because something utterly invisible like that does not form any idea in our thinking.

On hearing this, I was allowed to tell them that they did well to think of God in human form and that many people on our planet have similar thoughts, especially about the Lord. The early people on our planet thought that way too. I then told them about Abraham, Lot, Gideon, and Manoah and his wife, and what it says about them in our Word, namely, that they saw God in human form and acknowledged him as the Creator of the universe, calling him "Jehovah," and in their case as well this came from an inner perception. Today in the Christian world, though, that inner perception has [mostly] perished; it remains only among uneducated people who are devoted to their faith.

159 Before I said all this, they had believed that our group was another one intending to confuse them with the notion of God as three, so when they heard this they were moved with joy and declared that God (whom they now called "the Lord") had sent them people to teach them about himself.

They asserted that they are no longer willing to admit visitors who disturb them, especially with the notion of three persons in the Godhead, because they know that God is one and that there is only one Divinity; there is not a unanimity among three—unless we think of God as being similar to an angel. In angels, they explained, there is indeed an invisible core of life that enables them to think and be wise, a visible outer level of life in human form that enables them to see and act, and an emanation of life that is an aura of love and faith that comes from them. From every spirit and angel there emanates an aura of life by which they can be recognized at a distance.ᵃ In the Lord's case, this emanation of life from him is the divine nature itself, which fills the heavens and makes them what they are, because it comes from the true reality underlying the life within everyone's love and faith. They said that this was the only way they could conceive of a trinity and a unity at the same time.

[2] On hearing this, it occurred to me to say that this way of holding a trinity and a unity at the same time is in agreement with the way angels conceive of the Lord and also squares with what the Lord actually taught about himself: he taught that he and the Father are one, that the Father is in him and he in the Father, that whoever sees him sees the Father, and that whoever believes in him believes in the Father and knows him. The Lord also taught that the Comforter, whom he calls "the Spirit of Truth" and "the Holy Spirit," emanates from him and speaks on his behalf, not on its own authority; the Comforter means the emanating divine nature.

[3] I went on to say that this concept of a trinity and a unity at the same time is in agreement with the underlying reality and manifestation of the Lord's life when he was in the world. The reality underlying his life was the divine nature itself, since he was conceived by Jehovah and the reality underlying anyone's life comes from that by which it is conceived. The manifestation of that life from that underlying reality is what is human in form. The reality underlying our life that we get from our fathers is called the soul, and the consequent manifestation of life is called the body. The soul and the body together make one person. The relationship between the two is like the relationship between a force and a resulting action. The action is in fact the force at work, so the two are one. In us, what is referred to as our will is the driving force, and what are called our actions are that force at work. Our body is the instrumental element by means of which our will

---

a. See note g on §64.

acts, our will being the principal element behind it; and when we are doing something, the instrumental element (our body) and the principal element (our soul) are one. This is how the angels in heaven conceive of the soul and the body. Therefore they know that the Lord made his human nature divine from the divine nature within himself that was the soul he had from the Father.

The statement of faith that has been accepted throughout the Christian world is not in disagreement with this, since it teaches the following:

> Although Christ is God and a human being, yet he is not two, but one Christ. Indeed, he is one altogether, one person. Therefore as the body and the soul are one human being, so God and a human being are one Christ.[b]

Because there is this kind of union, this kind of oneness, in the Lord, he unlike anyone else rose from the dead not only with respect to his soul but also with respect to his body, which he glorified in the world. In fact, he taught his disciples this when he said, "Touch me and see, because a spirit does not have flesh and bones as you see I have" [Luke 24:39].[c]

The spirits readily understood this because spirits who are angelic find such concepts understandable. They then added that only the Lord has power in the heavens and that the heavens are his. I was inspired to say that the church on our planet knows this as well, from the mouth of the Lord himself before his ascension into heaven: he then said, "All power has been given to me in heaven and on earth" [Matthew 28:18].

160 Later I talked with the spirits about their planet, since all spirits remember such things when their earthly or outer memory is opened by the Lord. We bring such memories with us from the world, but they are opened only when it pleases the Lord.

Concerning the planet that these spirits had come from, they said that when they are given permission they become visible to people who are living on their planet and talk with them face to face. How this happens is that the spirits are brought into consciousness of their earthly or outer memory and therefore into the kind of thinking they had been engaged in when they lived in the world; at the same time the inhabitants

---

b. This is from the Athanasian Creed.
c. We rise in spirit immediately after death and are in human form; we are [then still] human in absolutely every respect: 4527, 5006, 5078, 8939, 8991, 10594, 10597, 10758. We rise from the dead in our spirit, not in our body: 10593, 10594. Only the Lord rose from the dead with his body as well: 1729, 2083, 5078, 10825.

of the planet have their inner or spiritual sight opened and see the spirits by means of it. They also said that for all the inhabitants know, the individuals they are seeing are also inhabitants of their planet; they first realize they are not when they suddenly vanish from their sight.

I told them that something like this happened on our planet in early times, to Abraham, for example, Sarah, Lot, the inhabitants of Sodom, Manoah and his wife, Joshua, Mary, Elizabeth, and the prophets in general. I said that the Lord looked like other people and that the people who saw him could not tell that he was not just another earthly individual until he revealed himself.

This rarely happens nowadays, though, so that events like this will not compel people to believe. Belief by compulsion, the kind induced by miracles, does not take hold; and it also would do harm to those people who are able to have belief implanted in them by means of the Word without any need of being compelled.

The spirit who had been a church leader and preacher in the world **161** had absolutely refused to believe that other planets besides our own could be inhabited, because while in the world he had considered that the Lord was born only on our planet and that no one can be saved without the Lord. Therefore he was put into a state like that of the spirits when they become visible as ordinary individuals on that planet, as described just above. This made it possible for him not only to see their planet but also to talk with some people there. Once this began, his perspective was shared with me so that I likewise saw the inhabitants, and other features of that planet as well (see §135 above).

We saw four kinds of people there, one after another. At first we saw a kind that wore clothes; then a kind that was naked, whose skin was of a flesh color; then another kind that was naked, but whose bodies looked inflamed; and finally a kind whose skin was black.

When the spirit who had been a church leader and preacher was with **162** the kind of people that wore clothes, a woman appeared who had a very pretty face, dressed in a simple garment with an outer layer draped becomingly across her back and over her arms. She had a beautiful head covering in the form of a garland of flowers. The spirit was entranced at seeing this young woman, and spoke to her and even took hold of her hand; but since she noticed that he was a spirit and not someone from her own planet, she abruptly pulled herself away from him.

After that he saw several other women to his right who were shepherding sheep and lambs. They were leading them to a watering trough that was supplied with water through a small channel from a lake. They were similarly dressed and had in their hands shepherds' crooks, with which they were leading the sheep and lambs to drink. They said that the sheep will go wherever they point with their crooks. The sheep we saw were large, with broad, long, woolly tails. We saw the women's faces nearer at hand; they had beautiful features.

We also saw some men. Their faces were the same color as the skin of people [in Europe] on our planet, but with the difference that the lower part of their faces was black rather than bearded and their noses were more snow-white than flesh-toned.

[2] The spirit—who, as already noted, had been a preacher in the world—was then taken to the next location, but unwillingly, because he was still thinking intently about the woman he had found so delightful. This was obvious because there was still a kind of visible shadow of him in the place where he had been.

He was brought next to the kind of people who were naked. He saw them walking in pairs, husband and wife, wearing loincloths and a kind of covering on their heads. Once the spirit reached them he was brought into the state he had experienced in the world when he felt the urge to preach. He said that he wanted to preach the Lord crucified to them. They, though, said that they did not want to hear anything like that, because they do not know what that means, but they do know that the Lord is alive. So then he said that he wanted to preach the living Lord to them, but this offer too they rejected, saying that they perceived something in his speech that was not heavenly, because he was motivated to do so mainly for his own sake and for the sake of his status and reputation; and they could tell from the tone of his voice whether he was speaking from the heart or not. Since he was that kind of person, they said, he could not teach them anything; so he kept silent. During his life in the world he had been an emotionally powerful preacher, so much so that he could move his listeners to a deep state of holiness. This effectiveness was acquired by artistry, though, and therefore came from himself and the world, not from heaven.

163 Further, they said that when in the presence of their own people, meaning the inhabitants who were naked, they could perceive whether they had a reverence for marriage or not. I was shown that they were able to perceive this because of the spiritual image they had of marriage. They explained this image as a compatibility of [two] inner selves formed by a bond between their goodness and truth—and so their love and faith; and they said that as that bond flows down into their bodies it becomes manifest as marriage love. This is because everything that has to do with our lower minds shows up in some earthly likeness in the body. So there is an earthly manifestation of marriage love when the inner selves of two individuals love each other and when because of that love each one longs to will and to think as the other one does. This means that they want to be together and to be joined to one another in the deeper levels of their minds. As a result of this, the spiritual feelings in their minds become earthly feelings in their bodies and clothe themselves in a sensory experience of marriage love. The spiritual feeling in their minds is a love for what is good and what is true and for joining the two together, because everything mental, everything having to do with thinking and willing, goes back to truth and goodness.

They also said that no marriage like this exists between one husband and more than one wife because the marriage of goodness and truth, which is a marriage of minds, is not possible except between two.

Then the spirit we have been talking about was brought to the people **164** who were naked but whose bodies looked inflamed and lastly to the ones whose skin was black, some of whom were naked and others of whom wore clothes. Each kind lived in a different part of that same planet, though. Spirits can be taken in a moment to different parts of a planet because they are moving and traveling not from one place to another, the way we do, but from one state of mind to another (see §§125, 127 above).[d]

Finally, I talked with some spirits of that planet about what people **165** on our planet believe about resurrection [immediately after death], saying that people from our planet cannot conceive of the idea that we come into the other life immediately after death and then look like people, with faces, bodies, arms, legs, and all our outer and inner senses, let alone that we wear clothes and have houses and homes. The sole reason for this is that most people on our planet base their thinking on their physical senses and therefore do not believe anything exists that they are unable to see or touch. Few of them can be lifted up from their outer senses to their inner ones and thus be raised into the light of heaven, in which we become aware of things like this. As a result, they are incapable of having any concept of their soul or spirit as human, only a concept of something like a formless breeze or air or breath that nevertheless has some life in it. This is why they believe they will be resurrected only at the end of the world, which they call the Last Judgment, and that then their bodies— even though they have disintegrated into dust and been scattered to all

---

d. See note a on §125.

winds—will be reassembled and united with their souls or spirits. [2] I added that they are allowed to believe this because people who base their thinking on their physical senses (as just noted) inevitably believe that the soul or spirit cannot live as an individual in human form unless it regains the body that it carried around in the world; so unless that body were said to rise again, they would reject from their hearts as incomprehensible any teaching about resurrection or eternal life.

[3] However, this thought about resurrection has one benefit at least, namely, that they do believe in life after death, and it follows from this belief that when they are lying sick in bed and not thinking as usual about worldly and bodily concerns, and therefore not thinking on the basis of their senses, then they believe they are going to continue living immediately after they die. At such times they actually talk about heaven and their hope of a life there as soon as they die, which has nothing to do with what is taught about the Last Judgment.

I went on to tell these spirits that sometimes I have marveled at the fact that when those who are part of the [Christian] faith talk about life and death and about people they know who are dying or have died but are not thinking at that moment about the Last Judgment, they believe their loved ones will live or are living as people immediately after death. But as soon as a thought about the Last Judgment comes into their minds, their view changes into a materialistic concept of the earthly body and its eventual reunion with the soul. [4] They are unaware that in our inner selves we are all spirits already and that this is what is alive in our bodies and in every detail of them: the body does not live on its own. For all of us, it is the spirit that gives the body its human form. We are primarily our spirit, and our spirit has a form similar [to a body]—a form that is invisible to physical eyes, but visible to the eyes of other spirits. That is why when our spiritual sight is opened, a process that involves our physical sight becoming inoperative, the angels we see look like people. To the ancients as well, as is described in the Word, angels looked like people.

I have occasionally talked with spirits I had known when they were living in the world and have asked them whether they would like to put their earthly bodies on again, as they used to think would happen. At the mere mention of the idea they ran far into the distance, stunned with amazement that in the world they had harbored such thinking out of a blind and mindless faith.

166   I also saw their homes on that planet. They were long low houses, with windows on the sides corresponding to the number of rooms into which they were divided. The roof was rounded, and there were doors at each end. I was told that these were homes made of earth, with sod roofs and windows made of fine grass woven together in such a way that light could shine through.

I saw children, too; the spirits said that neighbors would come to visit especially for the sake of the children, so that they could play with other children under the watchful eye of the parents.

I also saw fields that were turning white with grain almost ready for harvest. I was shown some seeds or grains of that harvest, which were like the grains of Chinese wheat. I was also shown some bread made from it, which was small, in square pieces.

In addition to this, I saw grassy fields with flowers there, as well as trees with fruits like pomegranates, and also bushes they had instead of grapevines that bore berries from which they made wine.

The sun there (which is a star to us) looks fiery to them and about a | 167 | quarter the size of our sun. Their year is about two hundred days, and their days fifteen hours, using the length of days on our planet for comparison. The planet itself is one of the smallest extrasolar planets, barely five hundred German miles in circumference. Some angels said this on the basis of comparable facts about our planet that they saw in me or in my memory. They reached their conclusions on the basis of angelic concepts that enable them instantly to know measures of space and time in true proportion to space and time in other locations. Angelic concepts, being spiritual, are vastly better in such respects than human concepts, which are earthly.

A Fifth Extrasolar Planet
and Its Spirits and Inhabitants

ON another occasion I was taken to a different planet in the universe | 168 | outside our solar system, and again this required a succession of changes of state, this time lasting almost twelve hours continuously.

Accompanying me were many spirits and angels from our planet. I spoke with them during our journey, or [spiritual] progression. We were taken now diagonally upward, now diagonally downward, but always toward the right, which in the other life is toward the south. I saw spirits in only two places along the way; in one of those I talked with them.

During our journey, our [spiritual] progression, it was granted to me to observe how vast the Lord's heaven for angels and spirits is. From the areas that are not inhabited I could tell that heaven is so vast that if there were millions of planets each of which had as many people as there are on ours, to eternity there would still be enough room for everyone to live in, and it would never be filled. I was able to deduce this by comparison with the size of the heaven that surrounds and serves our own planet, a size so relatively small that it does not amount to a billionth of the area that is uninhabited.

169 When some angelic spirits from that planet came into view they addressed us, asking who we were and what we wanted. We told them that we were travelers and had been brought there, and that they had nothing to fear from us. They were in fact afraid, though, that we might be more of the kind of people who disturb them about God, faith, and the like. It was because of people like this that they had retreated to the region of their planet that they were now in, to avoid such people in any way that they could.

When we asked what it was that had disturbed them, they said it was the idea that there are three [gods] and the notion that there is divinity but not humanity in God, when in fact they know and perceive that God is one and is human.

We could tell from this that the people who were disturbing them, the people they were avoiding, were from our planet. Another sign was that the only people in the other life who take journeys because they developed a passion for and delight in travel during their time in the world are the people of our planet. The people on other planets do not engage in travel.

We learned later that the visitors were monks who had traveled throughout our globe to make converts of non-Christians. We therefore told the spirits that they did well to avoid them because the monks' intention was not to teach but to amass wealth and gain power. Their first goal was to captivate the others' minds by various means; their second was to turn the others into their slaves.

We also said the angelic spirits did well not to let their own concept of God be disrupted by such people.

[2] They added that these visitors also disturbed them by saying that they should have faith and believe what they were being told; but they had replied to them that they did not know what faith was or why they would need to believe something when they could perceive in themselves whether it was true. These angelic spirits were part of the Lord's heavenly kingdom; all the people there have an inner perception that helps them recognize the truths that to us are matters of faith. Unlike people in the Lord's spiritual kingdom, they are bathed in enlightenment from the Lord.

We were also shown that the angelic spirits of that planet were from the heavenly kingdom by the flamelike light in which their mental images were presented. The light in the heavenly kingdom is flamelike; the light in the spiritual kingdom is a shining white.

When there is a conversation about matters of truth, people from the heavenly kingdom say no more than "Yes, yes," or "No, no"; they never resort to reasoning to determine whether something is true or not. They are the type of people the Lord is referring to when he says, "Let your communication be 'Yes, yes; no, no.' Whatever is more than these comes from evil." That is why they said that they do not know what it means to have faith or believe. In their eyes, this is like saying to friends who can see houses and trees with their own eyes that they should have faith or believe that there are houses and trees, when they can see them perfectly well. This is what people from the Lord's heavenly kingdom are like, and this is what these angelic spirits were like.[a]

[3] We told them that on our planet not many people have inner perception, because in our youth we learn about truths but we do not live by them. People have two basic abilities, called understanding and

---

a. Heaven contains two different kingdoms, one called the heavenly kingdom and the other the spiritual kingdom: 3887, 4138. Angels in the heavenly kingdom are immensely knowledgeable and are far wiser than angels in the spiritual kingdom: 2718. Heavenly angels do not think and talk the same way spiritual angels do, on the basis of faith, but on the basis of an inner perception that something is true: 202, 597, 607, 784, 1121, 1387, 1398, 1442, 1898, 1919, 7680, 7877, 8780. On the topic of the truths that belong to religious faith, heavenly angels say only "Yes, yes" or "No, no," while spiritual angels employ a method of reasoning to determine whether something is true or not: 202, 337, 2715, 3246, 4448, 9166.

will. Some people accept truths only into their memory and then to some extent into their understanding, but not into their lives—that is, into their will. Since people like this can have no enlightenment or inner vision from the Lord, they say that things must be believed or that we must have faith, and they also employ reasoning to determine whether things are true or not. They have no desire to perceive something by inner vision or by enlightenment of any kind flowing into their understanding. They say things like this because for them truths have no light from heaven, and to people with no light from heaven, things that are false can appear to be true and things that are true can appear to be false. As a result, a great blindness has afflicted many on Earth. Even though people do not practice what is true or live by it, they still say that we can be saved solely by our faith. It is as if we were human not because of and in accord with the way we live, but because of our knowledge of a type of faith that says it does not matter how we live.

[4] Later we talked with them about the Lord—about love for him, love for our neighbor, and regeneration—saying that loving the Lord is loving the commandments that come from him, which means loving to live by them.[b]

We said that love for our neighbor is wishing well to and therefore doing what is good for our fellow citizens, our country, the church, and the Lord's kingdom, doing so not for show or for credit for our own sakes, but because we care about what is good.[c]

On regeneration, we said that people who are being regenerated by the Lord and are putting truths straight into their lives develop an inner perceptiveness about truths, while people who accept truths into their memory first and only later will them and do them are people who are focused instead on faith. This is because they act on the basis of their faith, which they then call "conscience."

The angelic spirits said that they perceived that this was true and therefore also perceived what "faith" was. I expressed these things to them by means of spiritual images, which make it possible for things like this to be presented and grasped in the light.

---

b. Loving the Lord means living by his commandments: 10143, 10153, 10310, 10578, 10645.

c. Loving our neighbor is doing what is good, fair, and right in every task and in every function because we care about what is good, fair, and right: 8120, 8121, 8122, 10310, 10336. A life of love for our neighbor is a life in accord with the Lord's commandments: 3249.

The particular spirits I was talking to at the time were from the northern part of their planet. I was then taken to some others, who were from the western part. They too wanted to find out who I was and what I was like. They abruptly stated that in me there was nothing but evil; they thought that this would make me afraid to come any closer. I perceived, though, that this was the first thing they said to everyone who came to them. It was given me to reply that I knew perfectly well that this was true and that by the same token there was nothing but evil in them, because everyone is born into evil. Everything that comes from any people, spirits, or angels as a derivation of their own selves is nothing but evil because everything good that is in anyone comes from the Lord. They could tell from this that I was devoted to truth and gave me permission to talk with them.

They then showed me their mental image of the evil in people and the goodness from the Lord in them and how the two are kept separate from each other. They set them side by side, almost touching but still distinguished, yet seemingly connected in some indescribable way so that the goodness was leading the evil and reining it in to prevent it from acting impulsively. The goodness was thus leading the evil wherever it wished without the evil noticing this. This is how they presented the control that goodness has over evil while at the same time portraying a state of freedom.

[2] Then they asked me what the Lord looked like to the angels from our planet. I said that he appeared to them as a human being in the sun, enveloped there in the solar fire from which angels in the heavens get all their light. The heat that radiates from that sun is divine goodness, while the light from it is divine truth, and both come from the divine love that is the fire they see around the Lord in that sun. That sun is visible only to angels in heaven, though, not to spirits who are on a lower level, because spirits are less receptive to doing what is good out of love and to believing what is true than are the angels who are in the heavens (see §40 above).

They were inspired to ask about the Lord and how he appeared to the angels from our planet because it pleased the Lord at that time to make himself present to them and to restore order to the things that evil spirits had thrown into disarray there, the spirits they had been complaining about. In fact, the reason I had been brought there was to see this very thing.

Then I saw a dark cloud over toward the east coming down from above. As it descended it gradually looked brighter and brighter and came more and more into a human shape, eventually becoming a human form within a fiery ray of light surrounded by little stars of the same color. This was how the Lord made himself present among the spirits I was talking with.

All the spirits who were there flocked from all sides to that presence, and when they arrived the good were separated from the evil, the good to the right and the evil to the left. This happened immediately and seemingly spontaneously. The ones on the right were then arranged according to their particular type of goodness and those on the left according to their particular type of evil. The good were given a free hand to form a heavenly community for themselves, while the evil were cast into hell.

[2] Later I saw that fiery ray of light go down quite deep into the underground realm there, and as it did, the ray gradually changed, from fiery to transparent, then from transparent to murky, then from murky to opaque. I was told by angels that the way the ray of light looked reflected the receptivity of the inhabitants of that underground realm, either to truth that comes from goodness or to falsity that comes from evil; they assured me that the fiery ray of light itself did not undergo any changes whatever. They also said that both good and evil people live in that underground realm, but are clearly separated, so that the evil can be kept under control by the Lord by means of the good. They went on to say that from time to time the good are raised from there into heaven by the Lord and others then take their place; this goes on all the time.

In the course of the light's descent, the good were separated from the evil and everything was brought back into order. The evil had used deceptive arts of various kinds to infiltrate the homes of the good there and attack them. This was the reason for this visitation.

[3] The cloud that gradually looked brighter and came more and more into a human shape as it descended, eventually becoming a human form in a fiery ray of light, was an angelic community with the Lord at its center. This experience taught me what is meant by the Lord's words in the Gospels describing the Last Judgment: "He is going to come with angels in the clouds of heaven with glory and power" [Matthew 24:30; 26:64; Mark 13:26; 14:62; Luke 21:27].

172   Later I saw some monastic spirits, who had been traveling monks or missionaries in the world (the ones mentioned above [§169]); and I also saw a crowd of spirits from that planet, many of them evil, that the monastic spirits had attracted to their cause and led astray. I saw them in the eastern region of that planet, a region from which they had driven the good, who had made their way to the northern region mentioned earlier.

That crowd and the people who were misleading them were gathered into one group amounting to some thousands, and were then sorted out. The evil among them were cast into the hells.

I was given an opportunity to talk with one of the monks. I asked, "What are you doing here?"

He said, "I am teaching people about the Lord."

"What else?"

"About heaven and hell."

"What else?"

"That they should believe everything I tell them."

"What else?"

"That [I have] the power to forgive sins and open and close heaven."

We then explored what he knew about the Lord, the truths that belong to religious faith, the forgiveness of sins, our salvation, and heaven and hell, and it turned out that he knew hardly anything at all; on every topic he was in darkness and error. His sole obsession was a craving for wealth and power—a craving he had acquired in the world and had brought with him from there. I told him that since that craving was the reason he had come all the way to them, and since that is the type of teacher he is, he could not help but take the heavenly light away from the spirits of that planet and plunge them into the darkness of hell, bringing them under the control not of the Lord but of the hells. He was skillful at leading people astray, but stupid in matters concerning heaven.

Since that was the kind of person he was, he was then cast into hell. That is how the spirits of that planet were set free.

One of the other things the spirits of that planet said was that those visitors, the monastic spirits just mentioned, tried their best to persuade them to live together in a large community, not by themselves.

173

Spirits and angels live and dwell together after death the same way they had in the world. The ones who lived in large communities in the world live in large communities in the other life too, and the ones who lived in separate individual households or in extended families by themselves live that way there as well.

When these spirits were living on their planet they lived separately, household by household, extended family by extended family, and group by group; they did not even know what it would be like to live all together in one community. So we told them that the reason their visitors were persuading them to do this was in order to rule and dominate them and that this was the only way they could make them their subjects and slaves.

Their reply was that they have no idea what "ruling and dominating" even means. When I showed the city where I lived to one of the spirits who had come back with us, I discovered that those spirits would run away at the mere notion of being ruled over and dominated. The moment he saw the place he fled, and I never saw him again.

174 Then I talked with the angels who were with me about ways of exercising authority, saying that there are two basic ways of doing this, one out of a love for one's neighbor and the other out of a love for oneself. Authority exercised out of a love for one's neighbor is the kind that is found among people who live apart in individual households, extended families, and peoples, while authority exercised out of love for oneself is the kind that is found among people who all live together in one community. Among people who live apart in individual households, extended families, and peoples, the one who exercises authority is the father of the people, and under him are the heads of the extended families, with the parents of each household under them. The one called the father of the people is the one from whom the extended families have come, and the individual households have come in turn from these families, but the father of the people governs them all with the kind of love that parents have for their children. The leader teaches them all how to live, helps them, and shares as much as he can with them of what he has. It never crosses his mind to subordinate them to himself as subjects or servants. Rather, he loves them to obey him the way children obey their parents. Further, since as everyone knows this kind of love grows stronger as it extends to later generations, the father of the people acts from an even deeper love toward them than their own parents do. This is the kind of authority that is exercised in the heavens because it is how the Lord exercises authority. In the Lord's case, he acts and rules out of divine love for the entire human race.

[2] The exercise of authority that comes from love for ourselves, which is the opposite of the exercise of authority that comes from love for our neighbor, began when we alienated ourselves from the Lord. This is because to the extent that we do not love and worship the Lord we love and worship ourselves, and love the world as well. In order to be safe, it then became necessary for whole peoples, along with their extended families and individual households, to gather together and set up various forms of government. The reason for this is that the more self-love grew, the more evils of every kind increased, such as hostility, envy, hatred, vengefulness, cruelty, and deceit against everyone who opposes us. From the self-interest of people mired in love for themselves, nothing flows forth but evil, because our intrinsic

characteristics are nothing but evil; and since those characteristics are evil, they do not accept what is good from heaven. So when self-love rules, it becomes the parent of all such evils.[d] Then too, it is the nature of this love that to the extent that we give it free rein, it goes so wild that eventually each of us wants to rule over everyone else in the whole world, and each of us wants to own everything of value that belongs to others. Even this would not be enough: we want to rule over the entire heaven, as is quite clear from the present-day Babylon.

This, then, is the exercise of authority based on love for oneself, which is as different from that of a love for our neighbor as heaven is from hell.

[3] All the same, no matter how prevalent the exercising of authority from self-love is in communities or in kingdoms and empires, there is still an exercise of authority from love for our neighbor in them, in people who are wise because of their faith in and love for God, because such people love their neighbor. If the Lord's divine mercy sees fit, I will be explaining elsewhere that in the heavens individuals like this live among their own peoples, extended families, and households even though they are also together with others in communities. However, this is a function of being related to each other *spiritually,* that is, in terms of love for doing what is good and belief in what is true.

Later I asked those spirits about various things on the planet they came from, first about their worship of God and about revelation. On the subject of their worship, they said that the peoples and their families gathered in a particular place every thirty days and listened to sermons. They said that at those times the preacher, from a pulpit raised up a bit from the ground, taught them divine truths that were conducive to leading a good life. **175**

On the subject of revelation, they stated that this comes to them in the morning, in a state between sleeping and waking, when they are in an

---

d. Our intrinsic characteristics, which we get from our parents, are evil through and through: 210, 215, 731, 874, 876, 987, 1047, 2307, 2308, 3518, 3701, 3812, 8480, 8550, 10283, 10284, 10286, 10731. What is intrinsic to us is loving ourselves more than God, loving the world more than heaven, and regarding our neighbor as nothing in comparison to the self unless our neighbor is serving us and our own purposes, so it is a love for ourselves and for the world: 694, 4317, 5660. As long as love for ourselves and love for the world are in charge, they are the source of all evils: 1307, 1308, 1321, 1594, 1691, 3413, 7255, 7376, 7488, 8318, 9335, 9348, 10038, 10742. These evils are contempt for others, hostility, hatred, vengefulness, cruelty, and deceit: 6667, 7372, 7373, 7374, 9348, 10038, 10742. All falsity comes from these evils: 1047, 10283, 10284, 10286.

inner light that has not yet been interrupted by physical and worldly sensory input. At such times they hear angels of heaven talking about divine truths and about how to live by them; and later when they become fully awake, an angel dressed in white appears beside their bed, and then suddenly disappears from their sight. This is how they know that what they have heard comes from heaven. So they can tell the difference between visions from God and visions that are not from God: when the visions are not from God they do not see an angel. They added that revelations happen this way especially for their preachers, but sometimes for others as well.

176 When we asked about their homes, they said that they were low and made of wood, with a flat roof surrounded by a downward sloping rim. The husband and wife live in the front part of the home, their children in an adjacent room, and servants, female and male, at the back.

As for their food, they said that they drink milk with water and that the milk comes from cows that have wool like sheep. As for the way they live, they go naked and their nakedness is not a matter of shame to them. They limit their interactions to people within their extended families.

177 They told us about the sun of their planet, saying that it looks fiery to the people who live there. The duration of their year is two hundred days, and their days last just nine hours of our time—something they could tell by sensing in me the length of the days on our planet. Further, they said that it is always spring and summer for them, so their fields are in blossom and their trees bear fruit throughout the year. This is because their year is very short, amounting to only seventy-five days of our year; and where the years are that short, the cold does not last in winter or the heat in summer, so the soil is always fertile.

178 As for engagements and marriages on their planet, they told us that daughters are kept at home when they are near marriageable age and are not allowed to go out until the day when they are to be married. Then they are taken to a certain house of marriage where a number of other marriageable young women have been brought and stationed behind a platform that comes up to the middle of their bodies, so that their nakedness can be seen only from chest to face. Then young men come and choose wives. When a young man sees someone suitable for him, someone who appeals to him, he takes her by the hand. If she then follows him, he takes her to a home that has been made ready and she becomes his wife. They see from each other's faces whether their dispositions agree, because everyone's face there is a sign of his or her disposition. There is no dissimulation or deceit.

To ensure that everything happens properly and without lewdness, an elderly man sits behind the young women and there is an elderly woman to one side, both keeping watch.

There are many locations like this where the young women are brought, and there are also fixed times for the young men to make their choices. If they do not see a suitable young woman in one place they go to another, and if not at one time, they come back the next time.

They also said that a husband marries only one wife, never more than one, because this would be contrary to the divine design.

THE END

BIOGRAPHICAL NOTE

Biographical Note

E MANUEL SWEDENBORG (1688–1772) was born Emanuel Swedberg (or
Svedberg) in Stockholm, Sweden, on January 29, 1688 (Julian calendar). He
was the third of the nine children of Jesper Swedberg (1653–1735) and Sara Behm
(1666–1696). At the age of eight he lost his mother. After the death of his only older
brother ten days later, he became the oldest living son. In 1697 his father married
Sara Bergia (1666–1720), who developed great affection for Emanuel and left him a
significant inheritance. His father, a Lutheran clergyman, later became a celebrated
and controversial bishop, whose diocese included the Swedish churches in Pennsylvania and in London, England.

After studying at the University of Uppsala (1699–1709), Emanuel journeyed to
England, the Netherlands, France, and Germany (1710–1715) to study and work
with leading scientists in western Europe. Upon his return he apprenticed as an
engineer under the brilliant Swedish inventor Christopher Polhem (1661–1751). He
gained favor with Sweden's King Charles XII (1682–1718), who gave him a salaried
position as an overseer of Sweden's mining industry (1716–1747). Although Emanuel
was engaged, he never married.

After the death of Charles XII, Emanuel was ennobled by Queen Ulrika Eleonora
(1688–1741), and his last name was changed to Swedenborg (or Svedenborg). This
change in status gave him a seat in the Swedish House of Nobles, where he remained
an active participant in the Swedish government throughout his life.

A member of the Royal Swedish Academy of Sciences, he devoted himself to
studies that culminated in a number of publications, most notably a comprehensive
three-volume work on natural philosophy and metallurgy (1734) that brought him
recognition across Europe as a scientist. After 1734 he redirected his research and
publishing to a study of anatomy in search of the interface between the soul and
body, making several significant discoveries in physiology.

From 1743 to 1745 he entered a transitional phase that resulted in a shift of his
main focus from science to theology. Throughout the rest of his life he maintained
that this shift was brought about by Jesus Christ, who appeared to him, called him
to a new mission, and opened his perception to a permanent dual consciousness of
this life and the life after death.

He devoted the last decades of his life to studying Scripture and publishing
eighteen theological titles that draw on the Bible, reasoning, and his own spiritual
experiences. These works present a Christian theology with unique perspectives on
the nature of God, the spiritual world, the Bible, the human mind, and the path to
salvation.

Swedenborg died in London on March 29, 1772 (Gregorian calendar), at the
age of eighty-four.